JUST A THOUGHT AWAY

Just a Thought Away

Communicating With Loved Ones in Spirit

SHIRLEY SMOLKO, RN, CHT, GC-C

Joe Smolko, MEd., Editor

The Venetian Medium, LLC/Cavallaro Publishing

Published 2021 in the USA by Cavallaro Publishing

Copyright © 2021 by Shirley Ann Smolko
All rights reserved. No part of this book may be reproduced in any manner whatsoever without the express written permission of the author/publisher except for the use of brief quotations in a book review.

ISBN: 978-1-7345146-4-3

Library of Congress Control Number: 2021920490
A record of this book can be obtained from the Library of Congress in Washington, D. C.

Front & Back Cover Design by Shirley Smolko

First Printing in the USA by IngramSpark

DISCLAIMER

Before proceeding to read or use this workbook, you must agree and acknowledge that I am not providing any mental health advice in any way. The information provided herein is not mental health advice, and is not intended to be a substitute for professional Mental Health Services (including, but not limited to a psychiatrist, psychologist, therapist, counselor, etc.). Therefore, do not disregard or delay seeking professional mental health treatment for any mental health related issues you may be experiencing including, but not limited to, Post Traumatic Stress Disorder (PTSD) and/or Complicated Grief. If you have or suspect that you have a mental health problem, contact your own Mental Health Care Provider promptly. Also, be sure to reach out to your mental health provider with any questions you might have regarding mental health.

The information and techniques provided in this workbook are for educational purposes only and are intended as a self-help tool for your own use. There are no guarantees; your success depends primarily on your own effort, motivation, commitment, and follow-through. I cannot predict, and I do not guarantee that you will attain a particular result. By using this workbook, you accept and understand that results differ for each individual. Each individual's results depend on his or her unique background, dedication, desire, motivation, actions, and numerous other factors. You fully agree that there are no guarantees as to the specific outcome or results you can expect from using the information you receive from this workbook.

I dedicate this book to my husband and editor—Joe. His love, encouragement, and tenacious editing skills made this book possible. There was a time in our relationship before we were married when he told me he didn't believe in the afterlife, that when you're dead, you're dead. He's changed his mind!

ACKNOWLEDGEMENT

I would like to thank Spirit for suggesting I write this book. On a fall afternoon in 2020, I was walking down the Mind/Body/Spirit genre aisle at my local library when Dr. Louis. E. LaGrand's book *After Death Communication: Final Farewells* literally flew off the shelf and landed at my feet. There were no vibrations and I had not brushed up against the bookshelf. I stood there dumbfounded for a few moments just gazing at the book lying on the floor. As I bent over and picked up the book, a soft male voice clairaudiently spoke to me and said: *the bereaved need to know how to communicate with their loved ones, now more than ever.* I stood there with Dr. LaGrand's book in my hands and reflected on the fact that I had been asking Spirit to guide me in my next writing project.

CONTENTS

DISCLAIMER - v
DEDICATION - vi
ACKNOWLEDGEMENT - vii

~ 1 ~
After-Death Communication Is a Miraculous Therapy For Grief
1

~ 2 ~
In The Garden of Souls
9

~ 3 ~
The Physics of Spirit Communication
21

~ 4 ~
Is Spirit Communication an Evil Practice?
31

~ 5 ~
Programming Your Subconscious Beliefs for Spirit Communication
48

~ 6 ~
Types of After Death Communication
59

~ 7 ~
Understanding the Language of Spirit
69

~ 8 ~
Popular Ways to Continue Bonds
92

~ 9 ~
Coping With Grief
101

OTHER BOOKS BY SHIRLEY SMOLKO I - 115
OTHER BOOKS BY SHIRLEY SMOLKO II - 117

~ 1 ~

AFTER-DEATH COMMUNICATION IS A MIRACULOUS THERAPY FOR GRIEF

"Blessed are those who mourn, for they will be comforted."
—Matthew 5:4 KJV Bible

Popular Traditional Grief Theories

Every one of us will experience grief related to loss at some point in our lives whether it be the loss of a loved one through death or divorce, financial loss, or loss of good health. I think grief is best defined as an individual's response to loss, which may manifest physically, emotionally, cognitively, behaviorally, and spiritually. Simply put, grief is the price we pay for love, and a natural consequence of forming emotional bonds to people and possessions.

Grief therapy has undergone transformational change in terms of how the human experience of loss is understood and how the goals of therapy are achieved. Many long-held traditional views about the grieving process have been rejected because research has shown that they were not effective in treating grief. We are witnessing a significant shift away from the idea that successful grieving requires letting go of the deceased and are moving towards a recognition that maintaining continued bonds is a healthy response to grief. Recent research has failed to show that 'grief work' is critical to recovery. Also, the absence of grief is no longer viewed as being pathological.

Freud's Grief Work

The first major theoretical contribution on grief was provided by Freud in his paper "Mourning and Melancholia" (1917). According to Freud, 'grief work' involves a process of breaking the ties that bind the survivor to the deceased. Grief resolution involves three elements:

1. freeing the bereaved from bondage to the deceased,
2. readjustment to new life circumstances without the deceased, and
3. building new relationships.

Freud believed that the process of severing ties with the deceased is achieved by acknowledging and expressing painful emotions such as anger and guilt. The view was held that if the bereaved failed to engage with or complete their grief work, the grief process would become complicated, increase the risk of mental and physical illness, and compromise recovery. The grief work model stresses the importance of 'moving on' as quickly as possible to return to a 'normal' level of functioning.

Stages of Grief Processing

Over the years, several theorist have conceptualized grief resolution as proceeding along a series of predictable stages. Of these theorists, Elizabeth Kubler-Ross has the best-known model. Her model was initially used to help identify the stages of the dying patient before it was applied to the process of grieving experienced by the bereaved. Kubler-Ross's five stages are as follows: denial, anger, bargaining, depression, and acceptance.

Denial

Denial is a common defense mechanism that may help buffer the immediate shock of the traumatic situation. Initially, you may doubt the reality of the loss. You may even find yourself fantasizing that someone will call to say there's been a mistake and your loved one didn't die. At some point, you could feel as if nothing matters to you anymore. Life as you once knew it has changed, and you don't want to move on. The stage of denial is a temporary response that carries you through the first wave of pain.

Anger

During the anger stage of grief, you might ask questions like "Why did he have to die?" or "What did we do to deserve this?" You could also suddenly feel angry towards family members, friends, inanimate objects, pets, and even strangers. Anger toward the person who died is also a common response. Even when the death was through no fault of their own, you may resent them for leaving you. Anger is just one of many emotions you might experience during this stage. Anxiety, bitterness, impatience, irritability, and rage are just some of the other emotions you are likely to experience while trying to cope with your loss.

Bargaining

During this stage of grief processing, you may find yourself thinking of things you feel you should have done to prevent the death. It's also common to experience feelings of guilt as a result of thinking that you didn't do enough for the deceased. These thoughts and emotions are a normal response to grief during this stage.

Depression

During the depression stage, you start facing your present reality and the inevitability of the loss you've experienced. In this stage, depression is a natural and appropriate response to grief, and is not considered a mental illness. Common reactions to depression are:

- anorexia (lack of desire to eat),
- confusion and distraction,
- fatigue,
- inability to enjoy doing things that use to bring joy,
- not wanting to participate in activities of daily living, and
- lack of desire to move forward with life.

These reactions are usually temporary and occur as a normal response to grief. As overwhelming as it may feel, this stage is a natural and necessary part of the healing process.

Acceptance

Accepting the death of a loved one isn't necessarily about being content with what happened. It is more about how you acknowledge the loss you've experienced, and how you readjust your life accordingly. Depending on your experience, it might be understandable if you never accept the death. During this stage, some people want to interact more often with friends and family, as well as to form new and lasting relationships.

Worden's Theory of Mourning

This theory of mourning suggests that grieving should be considered an active process that involves engagement with the following four tasks:

- accepting the reality of the loss,
- processing the pain of grief,
- adjusting to a world without the deceased, and
- establishing an enduring connection with the deceased while embarking on a new life.

Accepting the Reality of the Loss

This task involves coming to terms with the death of a loved one. It is not uncommon to experience shock or disbelief following a loss, or feel as if you are living in a dream. You might continually look for your loved one to walk through the door, or to be on the other end of the phone when it rings. Many people believe acceptance is achieved just by surrendering to the reality of the death; however, there are some people who believe that acceptance is only achieved by severing ties to one's past with the deceased. From a clinical perspective, acceptance is thought to be achieved when an individual is ready to begin their journey of healing, and move forward with life.

Processing the Pain of Grief

Grief is naturally accompanied by a wide range of intense emotions such as anger, anxiety, confusion, emptiness, loneliness, longing, numbness, and sadness. This task of the grieving process is considered to be adaptive and involves working through these emotions. It has been said that the best prescription for grief is to grieve. There is no way to "get around" grief; we have to be willing to go through it to get to the other side. During this time, it is important to focus on good self-care such as eating well, getting physical exercise, sleeping, and spending time with others.

Adjusting to a World Without the Deceased

Soon after the death, you will start to resume your normal routine. Adults will have to either go back to work, and students will have to go back to school. During this time you realize the different roles and responsibilities your loved one performed. The task of readjustment can happen quickly or slowly over an extended period of time. Readjustment depends upon the number and extent of adaptations required to assume the roles and responsibilities left by the deceased loved one. Accomplishing this task may require learning new skills and responsibilities, such bill paying, doing laundry, living alone, and single parenting. This task also requires learning to identify available resources and asking for help when needed.

Establishing an Enduring Connection with the Deceased While Embarking on a New Life

This task includes finding an appropriate, ongoing connection in our emotional lives (either through continuing bonds, or severance of ties) with the person who has died. The goal of this task is to allow for our thoughts and memories of the deceased, while simultaneously engaging in activities that are meaningful and bring us pleasure. These activities may include new people or new relationships. Failure to accomplish this task is a failure to thrive, or move forward in life. It is vitally important for us to continue to live our lives with a sense of purpose and meaning and to remember that life did not stop when the person died.

While changing the fact that our loved one has died is impossible, we do have choices in how we respond. We could choose to stay immersed in sorrow, or we could choose to live our life to the fullest. Why do some individuals choose to wallow in sorrow? To some people it may feel like the strongest, most palpable connection they have left to their loved one. Also, it may feel as though they would be betraying or diminishing their love for them if they were to ever be happy in a world without them. I have lost a spouse, and I will not criticize those who feel this way. Neither will I criticize those individuals who choose to reorganize their life and live it to the fullest.

Continuing Bonds Theory

In contrast to earlier theories, continuing bonds theory focuses on an individual's need to continue a relationship with the deceased in a new and redefined way, changing from loving in physical presence to loving in physical absence. This new type of relationship helps the bereaved to cope with the physical loss. Communication is one of many natural and common ways to maintain a relationship with deceased loved ones. Research has repeatedly shown that the experience of communication with the deceased is not symptomatic of any mental disorder, but is actually therapeutic to the bereaved. There has been an ongoing movement away from the idea that successful grieving requires 'letting go' of the deceased. This idea represents recognition that death ends a life, not necessarily a relationship. Rather than 'saying goodbye' or seeking closure, there exists the possibility of the deceased being both present and absent for those individuals wishing to continue a bond.

A continuing bonds relationship with the deceased may be achieved by talking to the deceased, visiting their grave, initiating charitable scholarships in their name, or keeping objects, such as jewelry that belonged to them. The evidence of this continuing bond may be experienced in a variety of ways. For example, the deceased may interact with the bereaved in their dreams, by signs and symbols and through the sensing of their presence. Research has shown that nearly half of the bereaved population studied have sensed the presence of a deceased loved one. The true incidence is thought to be much higher because of reluctance among the bereaved to disclose its occurrence to clinicians due to fear of being ridiculed.

Clinically, much attention has been placed on attempts to distinguish the conditions under which continuing bonds is adaptive from those in which it is maladaptive. Growing evidence suggests that individuals who experience insecure styles of attachment are more prone to chronic grief trajectories, which contribute to maladaptive rather than adaptive forms of continuing bonds with the deceased. An important factor in distinguishing an adaptive versus maladaptive relationship to the deceased occurs when the continuing bonds expression reflects an attempt to maintain a physical bond with the deceased instead of a spiritual one. The goal in continuing bonds is to achieve a more internalized, symbolically based connection, which suggests a greater acceptance of the death.

Using After Death Communication to Continue Bonds

After death communication (ADC) is congruent with the continuing bonds model and allows the bereaved to heal grief through the life-changing experience of reconnecting with their deceased loved ones. Research has shown that it's not uncommon for the bereaved to experience some form of contact with the deceased. It has been estimated that roughly one-third of adults in the US have had after-death contact (LaGrand, 2005). Most spontaneous after-death communications (ADCs) are experienced during the first year following the death of a loved one. Many others take place, with decreasing frequency, within the second to fifth years (Guggenheim & Guggenheim, 1995).

In 1996, Dennis Klass, Steven Nickman, and Phyllis Silverman published *Continuing Bonds: New Understandings of Grief*. This book challenged mainstream thinking about grief by offering a radically new model for understanding and treating grief. The authors cite many clinical observations and research outcomes that report survivors who maintain a continuing bond with the deceased appear to be better adjusted psychologically throughout the grieving process. After death communication as a means to continue bonds is usually beneficial, comforting, and can provide encouragement, consolation, and reassurance to the bereaved. Dannenbaum and Kinnier (2009) found that experiences of communication with the deceased can alleviate grief and result in therapeutically beneficial effects including: feeling cared about and loved; experiencing resolution of grief and relationship conflicts with the deceased, experiencing increased confidence in problem solving and decision making. In addition to alleviating grief, after death communication provides relief in knowing that our loved ones live on.

ADCs occur across culture, race, age, socio-economic status, educational level, gender, and religious belief. Experts in the fields of bereavement, counseling, and parapsychology support the idea that ADCs are common, natural experiences, which most experiencers find comforting, encouraging, and sometimes even life-saving. ADCs usually occur spontaneously, but can also be intentionally induced and experienced by most individuals. In his co-authored book *What Is Consciousness? Three Sages Look Behind The Veil*, Ervin Laszlo writes:

> *Contrary to popular belief, it appears that contact and communication with the consciousness of a deceased individual does not require exceptional gifts or capacities. Apparitions, visions, and deathbed visitations have been reported throughout history, and discarnate beings were said to appear suddenly and communicate with ordinary people.*

Individuals who desire but have not experienced a spontaneous ADC (sADC) may turn to facilitated, assisted, or requested ADCs. Spontaneous ADCs occur unexpectedly and are uninvited. Facilitated ADCs (fADCs) are intentionally induced and occur during a specific established protocol with the direction of a trained facilitator. Assisted ADCs (aADCs) involve receiving messages from the deceased through a psychic medium who directly experiences the communication and shares the messages with the client, also known as the sitter. The term requested

ADCs (rADCs) refers to experiences that occur as the result of employing technological or other physical apparatuses, or by using psychoactive substances, such as Ayahuasca, which has harsh side effects. I personally do not approve of, nor do I recommend the use of any psychoactive substance or drug to induce spirit communication. It simply is not necessary and may cognitively diminish the enriching experience of spirit communication.

Although I mention other modalities of initiating communication with Spirit, the focus in this workbook is on using the RISCH™ (Rapid Induction Spirit Communication Hypnosis) method. My intent in creating this method is to demystify and simplify the process of spirit communication, and to demonstrate that anyone can experience dialogue with Spirit.

Once you have learned to achieve altered states of awareness, you will not only be able to perceive spirit communication, you will also be able to tap into and develop other psychic abilities, including but not limited to, clairvoyance, clairaudience, clairsentience, precognition, and remote viewing. I hope this workbook brings you much wisdom, insight, and an awareness of your higher self and true potential.

Exercise #1

How Do You Plan to Resolve Your Grief?

There are basically two main approaches to grief resolution: relinquishing the relationship or continuing the bond. Your grief work must resonate with you and your reaction to the death of your loved one. Once you have decided on whether to relinquish the relationship or continue the bond, you can begin the journey of coping with your loss, and restructuring your life in a meaningful way. If you choose to continue bonds with your loved one, then this workbook is definitely for you! With that said, you may decide later on in your grief work that you want to relinquish the relationship and let your loved one rest. There is no right or wrong way to grieve. In the spaces below, list two reasons for wanting to continue bonds with your loved one in Spirit.

Reason #1:
_____
_____
_____
_____

Reason #2:
_____
_____
_____
_____

Exercise #2

Have You Experienced Spontaneous After Death Communication?

Spirits attempt to communicate with us in a myriad of ways including but not limited to dream visitations, appearing as apparitions, producing smells associated with them (i.e., cigar smoke, perfume), touching you, manipulating electronics, and having you feel their presence. In the space provided below, please write about any instances of after death communication or encounters with Spirit you have experienced.

~ 2 ~

IN THE GARDEN OF SOULS

"You don't have a soul. You are a Soul. You have a body."
—C.S. Lewis

"In My Father's house are many dwelling places. If it were not so, I would have told you, because I am going there to prepare a place for you."
—Jesus of Nazareth (Amplified Bible)

We Are Eternal

We are eternal—well, at least the soul is. So, what exactly is the soul? According to what the spirits have told me over the years about their existence in the afterlife, they have a body, which they can mold and morph at will. For the most part they maintain an astral body that is identical to the physical one they had in life, but usually with improvements they have created while in spirit. For instance, if a gentleman was bald in his physical body, but desired to have a full head of hair then he might choose to manifest a full head of hair in his astral body. In this chapter I'll explain the most popular spiritual concepts about the soul and its abode, as well as what I've been told concerning their spiritual bodies and the dimensions where they live and travel to.

The Essence of the Soul

Death is simply the separation of the soul, or spirit, from the physical body. I prefer to use the word soul because I think it connotes the total essence of an individual spirit person. While still connected to the physical body, the etheric layer of the soul acts as a power source for the physical frame thereby animating it with vital life force energy. When this power source, or etheric layer, completely separates from the physical body, the soul is freed and the physical body begins to perish.

According to many eastern religious and spiritual philosophies, such as Hinduism, Buddhism, and Jainism, the soul is comprised of at least seven subtle bodies, which are layers of energy that are part of, and extend beyond the physical body. These layers, or subtle bodies, form an integrated system, which makes it possible for us to access higher multidimensional planes of consciousness, whether the soul is in or out of the physical body. There is quite a bit of variation in the popular literature concerning the actual number and categories of these subtle bodies, which can be very confusing; therefore, I will present what I feel is an accurate depiction of the soul. Instead of thinking in terms of the soul being made up of different subtle bodies, I like to think of these subtle bodies as being characteristics of one soul body. For the sake of simplicity, I will not treat the subtle bodies as if they exist on their own, because I don't believe they do. With the exception of the etheric body, I will treat the subtle bodies as being aspects of one astral body.

The astral body, which is composed of pure conscious energy, carries the core essence of who we are such as our personality, intellect, desires, likes and dislikes. This body continues to exist even after the death of the physical body. As I stated earlier, I do not like thinking of the soul as having different bodies; however, there is a special layer known as the etheric body, which I feel is worthy of mention because it seems to have a function that is uniquely different from the other bodies—it acts as a powerhouse of energy, which I believe animates the physical body while alive, and the astral body after death.

The etheric body, which is an exact replica of the physical body, links the physical body to the soul. Life-giving energy from the Creator, known as Prana, is drawn in through the etheric body, and distributed to the physical body. Prana, which is found in all living things, is the Sanskrit word for this vital force. Known as Chi in Chinese, and Ki in Japanese, and Mana in Polynesian, Prana has a consciousness of its own.

I believe the etheric body feeds the astral body with sustaining energy after the physical body dies. Physical death occurs when the cord connecting the ethereal body to the physical body is completely severed. Many astral projectors have reported seeing this cord and described it as being a silvery-white rope that attached their ethereal body to their physical body. I personally did not witness this cord during any of my out-of-body episodes. Apparently, I was so caught up in each of my experiences that I was oblivious about how I was connected to my physical body. As an interesting side-note, it's the ethereal body that energy healers work on to affect healing in the physical body.

Dimensions in the Garden of Souls

All spiritual beliefs state our soul goes somewhere after death—but where? In this section, I will briefly explain theories on the nature of the spiritual realms, which man may go to after death, as postulated in the doctrines of Theosophy, Swendenborgism, and Spiritualism. Then I will discuss what the spirits have revealed to me about their world.

Theosophists believe the soul is the center of individualized consciousness within the all-consciousness of the Universal Mind, and its latent God-like attributes are expressed through a mechanism of consciousness that is formed of the matter of the various spiritual planes. Seven primary planes with many sub-planes have been identified in theosophical literature. For the sake of simplicity, I will omit the physical plane and categorize the spiritual realms into five planes. I will also divide the astral realm into two sub-planes.

In Theosophy, the ethereal plane is the first realm of the spiritual dimensions. I like to think of the ethereal plane as being in the "real-time zone" because it is a direct and objective reflection of physical reality in real time with some properties of the astral dimension, such as a fluid landscape that is permeable. This real-time zone overlays and permeates the physical dimension and contains a perfect reflection of reality within it. Everything happens in real-time as reality actually happens. Out-of-body projectors traveling within the real-time zone will perceive themselves as following the actual spatial contours of the physical world, but with the ability to fly and pass through solid physical structures. Projectors can also travel anywhere in the physical universe at will, at any speed just by expressing their intent through thought. The experience is much like being a ghost because the newtonian laws of physics do not apply. At the time of this writing, I have experienced this plane of existence twice during spontaneous out of body projections.

The second spiritual plane is the astral plane. Unlike the ethereal plane, the astral plane is completely nonphysical. Although the astral plane consists of many different realms and layers within those realms, I believe it can be divided into into two main realms—the lower, and higher realms. Each layer within these realms vibrate at a different frequency with the lower levels vibrating at the lowest frequency and the upper levels vibrating at the highest frequency.

Lower Astral Realm

Between the ethereal and lower astral realms is a layer known as the abyss, which acts as a veil to conceal and separate the ethereal realm from the lower astral realm. This veil keeps spirits from the lower astral realm from moving down into the ethereal plane; however, higher beings can come down through it.

Hell was not intended for human souls, but most souls who find themselves in the lower astral realm upon death are usually filled with the same negative beliefs, emotions, thoughts, and feelings they had in physical life. The Law of attraction can draw situations and circumstances into our spiritual life just as it does in earthly life; however, anything we manifest by the law of attraction while in the spiritual realm will manifest quicker than it would if we were in the physical realm. Based upon our beliefs, extremely low frequency aspects of our conscious mind are responsible for manifesting our experience in the afterlife.

The lower astral realm may have very low light in some places and be completely devoid of light in others. This realm is also home to negative entities such as thought-forms called tulpas; servitors called golems who were created by man; and fallen angels called demons who were created by God, but fell from grace. These entities are grounded to this realm because of their low frequency.

Unlike a created entity or thought-form, a soul in this realm will eventually rise from the lower astral plane to the higher astral plane by raising their vibration. Souls can raise their vibration to a higher frequency by coming to an understanding of their human side, and why they committed certain acts. They finally enter a state of grace when they choose to love and forgive themselves for those acts. The hellish realms were never intended for the human soul. If a soul ends up there, it's because there are in a negative and destructive state of mind. The loving Creator offers love and grace to all who will accept it, but we must choose to allow ourselves to receive this love and grace by loving and forgiving ourselves.

As I write this section, I am reminded of a forty-seven year old male patient of mine who died from a heart attack while in our emergency department (E.D.); fortunately, the E.D. team was able to successfully resuscitate him. (You can find the complete story in my second book *My Adventures as a Psychic Nurse & Medium: Haunted Hospitals.*) After some testing, he was admitted to the cardiac step-down unit where I was assigned to do his pre-op and post-op teaching, as well as the prep for his CABG (Coronary Arterial Bypass Graft) surgery scheduled later that afternoon. As I hung his I.V. antibiotic, he told me about the after-death experience he had while in the E.D. I will not recount his whole horrifying experience here. Instead I will sum it up in his own words: "When I died in the emergency room, I went to hell, but was rescued by Jesus." His story was unlike any other I have ever heard from my patients. To him, hell was a real and horrifying place, but he knew in his heart that he didn't belong there. No human soul does!

It becomes easier to love and forgive ourselves when we acknowledge how our lower, or shadow selves can take control of and dominate our higher, divine selves. Like Christ, we are fully human, and fully divine. Praying for our loved ones in Spirit is another way to help them raise their vibration regardless of the plane they find themselves in. Communicating love and forgiveness to them is very comforting and therapeutic for them, and us.

Higher Astral Realm

The landscape of this plane is a lot like earth. The astral plane is where our consciousness resides between lifetimes. How we experience this realm (or any realm) depends upon our state of mind prior to death along with the beliefs we have about life after death. All of the astral plane is highly connected to emotional energy, and can even be shaped by it. This realm is what Christians refer to as Paradise, and Spiritualists refer to as Summerland.

A soul who passes into the middle astral plane upon death is met by friends and loved ones. Those with strong religious beliefs will be met by the religious figures of their religion. They will also be grouped with other souls who hold the same religious beliefs.

The Messianic Plane

Like Summerland, this realm is also a joyful place with beautiful earth-like vistas. The vibration here is much greater—there is a strong emotional perception of love and being one with God while still perceiving yourself as an individual spark of God. In this realm, you understand the unity of all things and recognize that love for another is actually love for yourself. Jesus taught from this plane.

The Celestial Plane

This is the plane where the entire universe connects at the energy level. The confines of the soul no longer exist, and you are connected to everything. It is a place of pure beauty, bliss, freedom, and unity. It is the seat of the Creator, and the center of all creation.

The Akasha Plane

Akasha is a Hindu word, which can be translated as sky, space, or ether. It is the space that fills the sky and connects everything within it. It could easily be referred to as the matrix of the universe. The akasha plane does not exist in any single specified space; it exist within and around everything.

Ether is the air filling substance that pervades the akasha, and acts as a medium of transmission, or communication. Considered the first natural element in Hindu philosophy, it gives birth to the other elements—earth, air, fire, and water. It is the substance or mana that provides the template for physical form, which is connected with the power behind all creation. This substance is the force behind every magical performance, religious or profane.

The Hall of Records exists on this plane. Originally called the Book of Life, it has also been referred to as the holographic archive of the universe. It contains a record of every event that has occurred in the physical world since its inception. In addition to past records, the akasha is said to contain the imprint of present and future memories.

The Spiritual World According to Swendenborg

Emanuel Swedenborg (16th century scientist, Christian mystic, theologian, and philosopher) describes creation as being made up of two separate, but coexisting worlds, the natural world, and the spiritual world. The natural world includes everything you see while in your physical body—trees, grass, flowers, the sky, houses, other people, your own body, and so forth. The spiritual world consists of the unseen realities like heaven, hell, and the world of spirits in between. Swendenborgians believe that all human beings arrive in the spiritual world as equals, regardless of their religious background, personal beliefs, nationality, gender, or race.

In the spiritual world, we have bodies, live in houses, enjoy community life, and are surrounded by plants, animals, and vistas like those of Earth. However, things work differently in the spiritual world. What we see is determined by what we are thinking. Individuals, and places are only as near or as far away as our thoughts of them. Thinking of a person or place can actually take you there. While the spiritual world might not seem very different from the natural world at first glance, it is actually a realm where our inner state of being (consciousness) is reflected in our surroundings.

When people first enter the spiritual world, they are often greeted by friends or relatives who crossed over before them. Spouses may be reunited, although not necessarily forever. Divorces are made in heaven as well as on earth. If two people were truly twin flames on earth, they may choose to live together as spouses in heaven too. Those who did not find love on earth will eventually find their perfect match in heaven—no one is ever alone unless they wish to be.

Swedenborg referred to the realm we enter immediately after death as the world of spirits. This is an intermediate realm situated between heaven and hell, and can be thought of as a "sorting out" zone from which spirits either go to heaven or hell. The Theosophist named this realm Summerland; however, it is also recognized as the place of the afterlife among Wiccans and other earth-based pagan religions. Swendenborg described three states (of consciousness) people might pass through in this realm.

In the first state, people are essentially the same as they were in life. They have all of their memories, beliefs and attitudes toward things, and they may even manifest the same surroundings that they had on earth. Swedenborg states this is why some people who have died aren't even aware they are in the spirit world, and may try to deny it if they are told that their physical body is dead. The spiritual world is a place where a person's inner nature becomes the whole of their being. This first state might last anywhere from a few hours to a year or more, depending on how long it takes for a person's outer nature (what they outwardly say and do) to harmonize with their inner nature (what they truly feel and believe). Anyone who has become totally transparent in this life, whether transparently loving or transparently hateful, is fully ready for either heaven or hell, and goes straight in.

In the second state after death, a soul becomes aware of the deeper parts of their inner nature. They act according to their inner values and are drawn to souls of like character. No "judge" passes sentences of guilt or innocence—we seek kindred spirits because that is where we feel at home.

There is a third state for people who are ready to go to heaven. It is a time for learning about heaven and how to lead a life that allows one to experience it. By this time, the soul is already in touch with the community in heaven where they will ultimately live, but may still have a lot to learn about their new community.

Swedenborg teaches that we are surrounded by the world of spirits, with heaven above us and hell below us; those in the highest heaven are closest to the Lord, while those in the lowest hell are described as being farthest away. Swedenborg described the Lord—who exists at the top of everything—as a living sun radiating divine good and truth throughout creation. While Swedenborg describes heaven as being a place of inexpressible joy and peace, he also states that people who are not ready to experience a certain level of heaven will feel uncomfortable, even sick, and will be forced to retreat back down to lower levels until they have been properly prepared.

According to Swendenborg, hell is the part of creation that is farthest from the Lord. Hell has different regions and levels just as heaven does. Since the Lord is the source of light and heat in the spiritual world, the deepest hells are also the darkest and coldest because they are the farthest from God. The only light and warmth that exists in hell arises from the fires of malice that emanate from its inhabitants. Souls who live in the deepest hells are the ones who embrace evil on the innermost levels of their being and find great delight in inflicting pain on others.

The popular Christian image of hell is one of fiery torment—a pit into which God casts sinners as punishment for their sins. The picture that Swedenborg paints is very different. He states that God does not judge or condemn anyone to hell in order to punish them. Also, there is no Devil who tortures sinners. It is the people in hell who torture each other by lying, manipulating and inflicting pain as they did when they were alive.

Correspondence Between the Planes

"As above, so below; As below, so above"
—*The Kybalion*

Hermeticism is a philosophical system that is based on the teachings of Hermes Trismegistus. Long before the days of Moses, Hermes Trismegistus, who is considered the master of esoteric knowledge, taught the "Hidden Wisdom" known as Hermetic philosophy. One of the concepts taught in this philosophy is called the Law of Correspondence. This law states that there is harmony, agreement, and correspondence between the planes of manifestation. All that is included in the Universe emanates from the same source, and the same laws, principles, and characteristics apply to each plane, or levels, as each manifests its own phenomena upon its own plane.

Law of Correspondences According to Theosophy

In *The Secret Doctrine*, Blavatsky wrote about the Law of Correspondences. This law, as noted in the Kybalion (a book published in 1908 on the Hermetic Philosophy of Ancient Egypt and Greece) states that the world above is the same as the world below and that the world below is the same as the world above, in other words, the physical world (microcosm) is a miniature copy of the spiritual world (macrocosm). Through the Law of Correspondences, a theosophist seeks to discover first principles underlying various phenomena by finding the shared idea.

The Law of Correspondence According to Swendenborgism

All things that exist in the earthly world and its three kingdoms—animal, vegetable, and mineral—correspond to those things in heaven. Every single one of our physical universes has a corresponding spiritual universe in heaven. That is, the things in the natural world correspond to the spiritual world because the natural world springs forth and subsists from the spiritual world. Both worlds emanate and subsist from the creative power of the Divine Mind, which if separated from it would perish and disappear. Every aspect of our earthly lives has a correspondence in heaven. We are able to talk to our loved ones in heaven because of the correspondence of communication.

As all things that are in accord with Divine order correspond to heaven, so all things contrary to Divine order correspond to hell. All things that correspond to heaven have relation to good and truth; but those that correspond to hell have relation to evil and falsity.

Spiritualist Beliefs About the Afterlife

Spiritualists believe when we make our transition into the realm of Spirit, we leave our physical form behind; however, our personality survives this and we continue to exist on the spiritual planes. We are still who we were in physical life, but without physical bodies. Heaven and Hell are not places to which we are destined to go, but states of mind of our own creation. Our place in the world of Spirit is determined by the Universal Law of Attraction, as our thoughts, words and deeds determine where we will be. In other words, we make our own Heaven or Hell by virtue of our thoughts, words and actions.

Spiritualists do not believe in a devil. They believe some souls have encased themselves with their own negative persona to the point where they find themselves in the hellish plane and must cleanse themselves of lower vibrational thought to rise to a higher plane. There is no eternal damnation because there is no absolute evil that can separate us from the Creator. Further, they do not believe in a vindictive God sitting in judgement over us. We are our own judges and we will receive compensation or retribution for whatever we have done, whether good or bad; however, we are given the opportunity to make spiritual progress and undo any wrongs we committed on earth. Spiritualists believe that we continue to grow and progress after we make our transition, as we choose to pursue growth. There is always more development open for us if we choose it.

What the Spirits Have Revealed to me About Their World

The spirits have told me that their world is created and experienced through the application of two laws—the Law of Attraction, and the Law of Manifestation. They explained to me that the Law of Attraction reflects back to us by default the energy we unintentionally project while the Law of Manifestation reflects back to us the energy we intentionally project. Both laws are based on the concept that energy follows thought and applies to both physical and spiritual realms of existence. Spirits can create whatever they want in the spirit world; all they have to do is think the thought of what they want and it will immediately manifest. They said that we can do the same thing in the physical world, but it takes longer.

During many of my mediumship readings, spirits will give me a glimpse of their otherworldly environment. Most of the landscapes I have been shown are beautiful earth-like vistas. Unfortunately, there have been a few occasions when I have witnessed dimly lit, gloomy looking vistas. The spirits in these gloomy looking vistas did not appear to be suffering. On the contrary, they seemed to be content and at home in their gloomy looking surroundings.

One night after going to bed I asked Spirit (God, Source, Creator, etc.) to show me the world of Spirit. As soon as I had fallen asleep, an olive complected man with black hair, dressed in a purple robe with a gold stole around his neck approached me. He had a bluish white light, which surrounded his head and body and emanated about three feet around him. This saintly looking man introduced himself as Paolo—my teacher and fellow light-worker. He took my hand and said that the world of spirit is created by thought, then he proceeded to show me that world. This is what I dreamed:

Immediately I found myself thrown into total darkness, which swirled around me like an icy cold black velvet blanket. I asked Paolo to explain why I was experiencing such a horrible cold and dark place. He told me it was the Abyss—a deep dark pit in the lowest realm of hell where pure evil is cast into and bound for all eternity. He said for me not to worry, only entities that are of the purest evil reside in the pit. These entities include spiritual beings such as tulpas and golems who were intentionally created by evil men to be spiritual servants, and demons who were originally created by God to serve mankind, but instead chose to rebel against God's creation. These demons despise mankind and are intent on wreaking havoc and causing destruction to the human race. The physical world belongs to human beings and only human souls have the right to create in the earth realm. Demons try to usurp this right by influencing mankind to commit evil deeds. Paolo said that human souls do not come here for eternity. Only the evil entities that worked through human souls to create destruction are sent here while the human soul is eventually rescued and set free.

Next, I found myself walking along what seemed to be a dirt pathway. I was engulfed in a gray, misty fog that felt wet and cold. Once in awhile, I could make out the silhouette of another human being or hear the sobbing of someone off in the distance. I asked Paolo where I was, and he said that I was in a realm of hell where extremely depressed souls go to immediately after death. I told him that I didn't think that was fair. He smiled at me and said that everyone of these souls were there because of their own vibration, and that they would only be there a short period of time before being rescued and taken to the healing hospital in Paradise, which is also known as Summerland.

Almost immediately I found myself standing in the middle of what looked like a huge hospital ward with rows of white metal hospital beds lined-up on each side. The hospital ward looked different from any I had ever seen. It appeared to be a Grecian palace with no exterior or interior walls, only tall columns that extended from the floor to the ceiling all the way around the huge rectangular room. All types of beautiful, colorful mosaics designed with glittering gemstones adorned the floor. The white gossamer draperies hanging between each column billowed in the breeze. The distinct scents of lavender, jasmine, and gardenias filled the air. I realized these were my favorite fragrancies, and then it occurred to me that each soul here experiences the scents they enjoyed the most while in the physical ream. The spirit patients, who were dressed in white clothes, appeared to be socializing and conversing with one another. I heard a lot of joyous laughter and singing. I remember thinking to myself, *what a drastic transformation these patients had experienced-from deep depression to complete and utter joy.* Paolo told me that most of the patients here were ready to be discharged to their new home in a community of their choosing where they would find meaningful relationships, and activity.

I asked Paolo to show me the communities. He took my hand and suddenly I found myself in the middle of a beautiful garden surrounded by mansions of every architectural design imaginable. I looked around and noticed that each mansion had a pool, as well as a tennis and basketball court. Every type of flower, shrub, and tree imaginable existed in this garden, along with all kinds of birds, butterflies, buzzing bees (by the way, I was told the bees don't sting!), and all kinds of animals—big and small. Spirit people were everywhere, some jogged and rode bikes through the park while others took leisurely strolls, or sat on benches made of gold and conversed with one another. I asked Paolo where God and the angels were. He said that God's throne and the angels exist in the celestial realm, which was two planes higher, but close enough to provide bright light for Summerland. He explained that the countenance of the Creator is the light that illuminates the heavenly planes where there is no darkness or night. Once again, he took me by the hand, and wisped me away to another plane.

Instantly, we were standing in the courtyard of a grand palace. The courtyard was filled with marble statues of animals, fragrant flowers, shrubs, and trees of every variety. This place had the same grandeur as Summerland; however, whereas Summerland felt more like a plane of leisure, this plane felt like it was more about purposeful activity. I asked Paolo why this plane seemed to be a place of purposeful activity. He told me that we were in the plane of the Masters who worked to create new worlds, heal old worlds, and intervene in special matters of existing worlds, such as the resolution of war and illness so that races, and species may survive. He said that we were standing in front of the Celestial Curia—the Great Senate House of the Universes.

We turned and walked up a few marble steps to the entrance of this grand building. Heavy doors that seemed to be made of solid gold automatically opened so we could enter. We were greeted by a tall humanoid entity with six wings; he was dressed in a white robe with a silver sash around his waist. His feet were clad with sandals that matched the color of his sash. He introduced himself to me as Seraphiel, a security guard in the order of the Seraphim.

He acknowledged and embraced Paolo with a hug and said, "Welcome St. Paul, it's good to have you back. I know you have been busy with many special assignments, but the council of Elohim will be expecting you to take your seat soon for a vote on the next phase of creation."

I looked at St. Paul in amazement and thought to myself, *is this actually the St. Paul of the New Testament?*

He apparently heard my thought and replied, "Yes. It is I. Also known as Saul, and known by you as Paolo. We must hurry now; we have one more plane to visit." He took my hand, and for the final time, we were on our way to another plane.

Immediately, I found myself riding on a fluffy white cloud with Paolo. We seemed to be ascending higher and higher. There were beautiful angelic looking beings riding up and down on their own cloud as if on an elevator, as well as fairy-like beings who flapped their wings to move about through the air. I asked Paolo where we were going. He told me that we were on our way to the throne of God, also known as the Spirit of All Creation. The light emanating from the throne seemed to get brighter as we rose higher, but it didn't hurt my eyes. In the background, I heard a symphony playing classical music. Periodically, I also heard what sounded like thunder. I asked Paolo why there was thunder in heaven. He said that it was the voice of the Creator. We finally stepped off our cloud and onto what looked like a sea of glass. I looked up and saw many structures that looked like cathedrals made of crystal. In the center of these cathedral was a huge throne made of solid gold and embellished with fine gemstones. Sitting on the throne was a huge ball of brilliant light. This ball of light contained seven different faces. I thought to myself, *these must be the faces of the seven spirits of God.* There were twenty-four thrones behind the main throne of God. I asked Paolo why there were other thrones. He said that the other thrones belong to the Elohim—the senators of the Celestial Curia—who sit upon these thrones when it is time to create or intervene in matters of the Universes. I told Paolo that I had been taught in church that God's throne was the only throne in heaven. He laughed and said, together we are the Elohim, we are one with God, including you, and God is one with us. Suddenly I remembered the following verses found in John 17:22-23 of the International Standard Bible:

> *I have given them the glory that you gave me, so that they may be one, just as we are one. I am in them, and you are in me. May they be completely one, so that the world may know that you sent me and that you have loved them as you loved me.*

I asked Paolo if God or the Elohim decided on the judgment of mankind. He said that neither God, nor the Elohim sends anyone to heaven or hell. That decision is made by each individual in accordance with their state of consciousness and the Law of Attraction. The Law of Attraction basically states that like attracts like. If your state of consciousness is one in which you are feeling happy, enthusiastic, appreciative then you are sending out positive energy. On the other hand, if you are feeling anxious, stressed out, angry, resentful, or sad, you are sending out negative energy. Source energy (God) will respond enthusiastically to either one of these vibrations. It doesn't decide which one is better for you, like a mirror it reflects back to you the image of the energy you are emitting, so you get more of what you're putting out. I asked him how it was possible for mankind to be rescued from lower vibrational frequencies. He said that when a soul calls out for help, they will receive grace. Grace is the energy that raises a soul's vibration and sets them free. The Master Christ descended to earth to teach and embody the energy of grace. He is one of the Elohim who sits on the throne.

I began to feel extremely overwhelmed by what I was seeing, and hearing. I remember waking up and looking over at my alarm clock. The digital face of the clock read 1:11. It was then that I realized I actually had a spiritual encounter. I thought to myself, *three ones, really? Three is the number of the Holy Trinity—one in three, and three in one. Wow!*

Exercise #1

It has been estimated that between 9 and 18 percent of people who have died and been resuscitated, reported having a NDE (near death experience). In many of these reports, some people said they got a glimpse of the afterlife. The experiences shared by people who have had NDEs are intriguing.

Have you had a NDE that gave you a glimpse into the afterlife? If so, write about it in the space below if not, do you believe it's possible to get a glimpse of the afterlife during a NDE? Speculate on why it may be possible.

_____
_____
_____
_____
_____
_____
_____
_____

Some loved ones and caregivers of dying patients undergo a type of end-of-life phenomena known as a shared death experience or SDE. During a SDE, an individual shares the death and transition experience with the deceased. This phenomenon is not controlled, and happens spontaneously without any effort on the part of the passive observer. Have you had a shared death experience? If you have, please write about it in the space below. If not, speculate on whether or not it's possible.

_____
_____
_____
_____
_____
_____
_____
_____

~ 3 ~

THE PHYSICS OF SPIRIT COMMUNICATION

"The Universe is Mental—Held in the Mind of THE ALL."
—THE KYBALION

How Is Spirit Communication Possible?

I believe spirit communication occurs through the mental transference of concepts and ideas from the mind of a discarnate (deceased) spirit to the mind of an incarnate (living) spirit, and vice versa. The Kybalion states that the universe and all it contains is a mental creation of THE ALL (God), and that THE ALL is SPIRIT. It also states that we are justified in thinking of Spirit as Infinite Living Mind (pp. 40-43, Three Initiates). The teachings in this book are thought to have come from Hermes Trismegistus who is said to have brought esoteric knowledge to ancient Egypt. The concept that God is Spirit is also found in the Bible. John 4:24 states:

> *God is Spirit, and those who worship Him must worship in spirit and truth.*

If Spirit is Infinite Living Mind, then it can be deduced that each individual spirit, whether in a physical body or a spiritual body, is also a living mind.

For over two thousand years there has been an ongoing debate as to whether or not the brain is the same thing as mind. They are often used interchangeably, but they are not the same thing. For example, the lungs are the organ for air, but the lungs are not air. In the same way the brain is the organ for the mind, but it's not mind. The following online definitions may also help to clarify the differences between brain and mind. The definition of brain at dictionary.com states that the brain is:

1. The part of the nervous system in vertebrates that is enclosed within the skull, is connected with the spinal cord, and is composed of gray matter and white matter. It is the control center of the central nervous system, receiving sensory impulses from the rest of the body and transmitting motor impulses for the regulation of voluntary movement.
2. The brain also contains the centers of consciousness, thought, language, memory, and emotion.

I prefer the definition of brain at Merriam-Webster.com, which basically defines the brain as a portion of the central nervous system that controls bodily movement, and integrates and processes sensory information from inside and outside the body. There is no reference to the mind, or consciousness being localized to the brain. Merriam-Webster's definition states that the brain is:

1. The portion of the vertebrate central nervous system enclosed in the skull and continuous with the spinal cord through the foramen magnum that is composed of neurons and supporting and nutritive structures (such as glia) and that integrates sensory information from inside and outside the body in controlling autonomic function (such as heartbeat and respiration), in coordinating and directing correlated motor responses, and in the process of learning.
2. A nervous center in invertebrates comparable in position and function to the vertebrate brain.

The definition of mind at dictionary.com states that mind is:

1. The element, part, substance, or process that reasons, thinks, feels, wills, perceives, judges, etc.: the processes of the human mind.
2. The totality of conscious and unconscious mental processes and activities.

I also like the definition at Merriam-Webster.com; it states that mind is:

1. The element or complex of elements in an individual that feels, perceives, thinks, wills, and especially reasons
2. The organized conscious and unconscious adaptive mental activity of an organism

From the above definitions of mind, we can conclude that the mind is not the brain, but the conscious and unconscious mental activity and processes that allows us to perceive, will, feel, think, reason, and judge.

Dr. Thomas Fuchs, researcher and professor of psychiatry and philosophy at the University of Heidelberg, makes the following comments about the brain in his article entitled *The Brain—A Mediating Organ* in the January 2011 edition of the *Journal of Consciousness Studies:*

> *The brain is certainly a central organ of the living being, but it is only an organ of the mind, not its seat. For the mind is not located in any one place at all; rather, it is an activity of the living being which integrates at any moment the ongoing relations between brain, body and environment. Assuming such an embodied, extended and dynamic view of the mind, the brain loses its mythological powers and turns into a still fascinating, yet far more modest mediator of human experience, action and interaction.*

In his paper, *On the Relation between the Mind and the Brain: A Neuroscience Perspective*, Edmund T. Rolls—a neuroscientist and professor at the University of Warwick—likens the brain to computer hardware, and the mind to computer software:

> *The relation between the mind and the brain is the mind-brain or mind-body problem. Do mental, mind, events cause brain events? Do brain events cause mental effects? What can we learn from the relation between software and hardware in a computer about mind-brain interactions and how causality operates? Neuroscience shows that there is a close relation between mind and matter. My view is that the relationship between mental events and neurophysiological events is similar (apart from the problem of consciousness) to the relationship between the program running in a computer and the hardware of the computer. In a sense, the program (the software loaded onto the computer usually written in a high-level language such as C or Matlab) causes the logic gates (TTL, transistor-transistor logic) of the hardware to move to the next state. This hardware state change causes the program to move to its next step or state. Effectively, we are looking at different levels of what is overall the operation of a system, and causality can usefully be understood as operating both within levels (causing one step of the program to move to the next), as well as between levels (e.g., software to hardware and vice versa). This is the solution I propose to this aspect of the mind-body (or mind-brain) problem.*

Thus far, I have attempted to illustrate with examples the differences between brain and mind, but I haven't talked about consciousness. What exactly is consciousness? Is it the same thing as mind? To help us answer these questions, once again, we'll start with the definition.

Dictionary.com defines *consciousness* as:

1. The state of being conscious; awareness of one's own existence, sensations, thoughts, surroundings, etc.
2. The thoughts and feelings, collectively, of an individual or of an aggregate of people: the moral consciousness of a nation.
3. Full activity of the mind and senses, as in waking life: to regain consciousness after fainting.
4. Awareness of something for what it is; internal knowledge: consciousness of wrongdoing.
5. Concern, interest, or acute awareness: class consciousness.

6. The mental activity of which a person is aware as contrasted with unconscious mental processes.

Merriam-Webster.com defines *consciousness* as:

1. The quality or state of being aware especially of something within oneself
2. The state or fact of being conscious of an external object, state, or fact
3. Awareness
4. The state of being characterized by sensation, emotion, volition, and thought: **Mind.**
5. The totality of conscious states of an individual
6. The normal state of conscious life
7. The upper level of mental life of which the person is aware as contrasted with unconscious processes

As you can see, both definitions make reference to consciousness as being an awareness of the mind. Simply stated, it is an awareness of both internal and external stimuli. States of consciousness can be divided into two main categories—normal waking consciousness, and altered states of consciousness. If we look at consciousness as being on a continuum, normal waking consciousness falls within the middle of the spectrum with heightened awareness on the higher end, and decreased awareness on the lower end. Normal waking consciousness is the walking, talking awareness we experience in carrying out activities of daily living.

A heightened state of awareness is a relaxed, but highly focused state of consciousness. Mystics experience ecstatic visions and union with "God" while in this state. This focused state of consciousness can be achieved through hypnosis, meditation, or just by setting the intention to do so. Heightened, or focused awareness is also the state necessary for manifesting. While in this state of consciousness, it is possible to become focused to the point where you become totally unaware of all external stimuli (deep trance).

A lower state of consciousness is simply decreased awareness to external stimuli. There are different degrees of awareness within the lower state of consciousness, such as daydreaming, dreaming, lethargy, stupor, and coma. When we daydream, we are in touch with the creative part of our mind at play. The state of awareness we experience during sleep allows us to meet with our deceased loved ones, and to travel in the astral realm while we dream. Even while we dream, we can still process and perceive external stimuli, such as a hot or cold room. Lethargic and stuporous states of consciousness may be due to sleep deprivation or the influence of drugs. A coma may be medically induced or experienced as the result of trauma to the brain. Someone in a coma may have out-of-body or near death experiences. In his book *Proof of Heaven,* Eben Alexander, MD, writes about his journey into the afterlife while in a coma. Dr. Alexander's experience is a prime example of the nonlocal consciousness we have access to even when the brain centers for external awareness are severely damaged.

The Three States of Consciousness According to Freud & Jung

Sigmund Freud divided human consciousness into three levels of awareness: the *conscious*, *preconscious*, and *unconscious*. Each of these levels corresponds to and overlaps with his concept of the id, ego, and superego. The conscious level consists of all the things we are aware of, including things that we know about ourselves and our surroundings. The preconscious consists of things we could pay conscious attention to if we wanted to, and where many of our memories are stored for easy retrieval. The unconscious consists of those things that are outside of conscious awareness. Much of what is stored in the unconscious is thought to be unpleasant or conflicting such as memories and feelings associated with childhood trauma, or inappropriate sexual impulses. Although these thoughts or impulses are stored out of our awareness, they can still influence our behavior.

Carl-Gustav Jung's (1875-1961, Swiss psychiatrist and psychoanalyst who founded analytical psychology) regarded the psyche as made up of a number of separate but interacting systems. The three main ones were the ego, the personal unconscious, and the collective unconscious. According to Jung, the ego represents the conscious mind, which includes the thoughts, memories, and emotions a person is aware of. The ego is the conscious awareness we have about ourselves and our identity. Like Freud, Jung emphasized the importance of the unconscious in relation to personality traits. However, he postulated that the unconscious consists of two layers, not one. He referred to the first layer as the personal unconscious, which is essentially the same as Freud's version of the unconscious. The personal unconscious contains temporality forgotten information and well as repressed memories. The second layer of the unconscious mind is called the collective unconscious. The collective unconscious is a universal version of the personal unconscious, holding mental patterns, or ancestral memory traces, which are shared with other members of human species. Jung referred to these ancestral memories as archetypes, which are represented by universal themes in various cultures, and are expressed through literature, art, and dreams.

Eddington's and Jung's Quantum View of a Conscious Universe

In the 1930s, Sir Arthur Stanley Eddington, a prominent British astrophysicist, was one of the first physicists who searched for aspects of consciousness in the universe. After years of research, he concluded that the universe is of the nature of a thought or sensation in a universal Mind. His ideas about consciousness are validated by quantum phenomena, which demonstrates that there is a conscious subatomic world we can't see with the naked eye. This subatomic world is a background of potentiality, that doesn't consist of things, but of forms. These forms are thought-like, not thing-like, and they are real because they can manifest in the physical world. The physical world emanates out of the subatomic realm of invisible forms.

Carl Jung's beliefs about the nature of consciousness are also in agreement with those held by Eddington. Jung believed that even though quantum forms are invisible to the naked eye, they are real because they have the potential to influence events and appear in the physical world. Jung received a schooling in quantum physics from his patient Wolfgang Pauli. Wolfgang was an Austrian Physicist who sought out Jung for psychotherapy for excessive drinking after his divorce in 1930. During his sessions with Pauli, Jung learned about a property called entanglement—how measuring the state of one particle seemed to instantly influence the state of another. Jung coined the term synchronicity to describe how entanglement influences our dreams, thoughts and behaviors. Simply stated, synchronicity states that events in the internal world, such as our thoughts, feelings and dreams are causal factors in the external world, in other words, external events are caused by internal factors, not external ones. Through this concept, Jung was attempting to remove the superstition and fantasy which surround unpredictable and impressive events, and to present a scientific rationale based on quantum physics. The theory of Synchronicity provides an argument for the workings of a great unseen power, which underlies the deep connection between psychic and physical events. This deep connection is the realm, or sub-strata of reality which lies beyond the material world. As a result of his interactions with Jung, Pauli was led to consider mind and matter as complementary aspects of the same reality.

In their academic research paper *Near-death Cases Desegregating Non-Locality/Disembodiment via Quantum Mediated Consciousness: An Extended Version of the Cell-Soul Pathway* Contain Pereira & J Shashi Kiran Reddy write about a near-death experience, which was verified by emergency department nurse Kimberly Clark. This was what she experienced that day:

> *One morning, as part of her daily work schedule at the Harbour View hospital, she was working with a team of doctors who were trying to save a woman who had been bought to the intensive care ward as she was suffering a massive heart attack. As the doctors tried to save the woman, her heart stopped several minutes; she was clinically dead for those few minutes and it was a miracle that the doctors could bring her back. When the woman calmed down she explained to Kim, that during her resuscitation she had found herself at the ceiling level and could accurately point at the corner of the room from where she was observing her own resuscitation. But this was not all; she had also felt herself three stories above the ground from where she could see a tennis shoe sitting on a ledge. The tennis shoe was dark blue, worn with a scruff by the little toe and the lace going under the shoe heel; she felt agitated because she wanted someone to get the shoe.*

When Kim checked the ledge of the patient's window there was no shoe, but when a through search of all the ledges in the hospital was conducted, on the opposite side of the hospital on a different floor, in a room with a window facing to the west there was a tennis shoe on the ledge with the same description that had been provided by the woman. Kim could not believe her eyes as she opened the window and reached down and picked up the shoe which bore the scruff on the opposite side. There were no other buildings on that side of the hospital and the details of this shoe as described by the woman could definitely not have been seen from the ground or from anywhere inside the hospital. To add to that, it was the first time that this woman had ever visited this hospital. To know that a shoe is lying on the ledge with its nearly perfect description, she should have either seen the shoe before the operation or she should have been there in the same room much before the operation, as there was no possibility of viewing the shoe from an opposite building. Then how did she see this shoe and experience its pattern and color especially during a situation when she was dead? Hovering above her body and viewing the shoe from three stories high was possible only if she was suspended from that height or if she was flying."

This near-death experience, and many other like it, reveals the empirical reality of nonlocal consciousness. Dr. Larry Dossey, M. D. said the following about nonlocal consciousness in his article, *The Nonlocal Mind*:

> *Human consciousness is fundamentally nonlocal—not localized or confined to specific points in space, such as brains and bodies, nor to specific points in time, such as the present. A mind that is nonlocal is unbounded in space and time, and cannot be separate from other minds, but must be united with all other minds. Unbounded minds would therefore form what I've called the One Mind. Our concept of mind has been expanding for some time. In the nineteenth and twentieth centuries, we were introduced to several subdivisions of mind—the conscious, preconscious, subconscious, unconscious, the collective conscious, and collective unconscious. The One Mind is an additional perspective but it is not a subdivision. It is the overarching, inclusive dimension to which all the mental components of all individual minds belong.*

Nonlocal mind is associated with nonlocal mental experiences. For instance, individuals may know things remotely, even at global distances. In studies testing this premise, the against-chance odds are millions to one. They may know future events, either consciously or unconsciously. They may successfully direct healing intentions to distant individuals who are in need, or mentally influence the healing rates of wounds in animals. Individuals may acquire detailed information about scenes and situations at global distances. These phenomena all reveal an aspect of consciousness that transcends physical confinement. In their academic article *The Nonlocal Universe,* Lowhrey & Bruce (2020) state the following regarding nonlocal mind:

> *Nonlocal realism is closely related to the view espoused by Erwin Schrödinger that the overall number of minds within the universe is just one. He went further by suggesting that mind has erected the physical outside world out of its own mental stuff. The interconnected universal consciousness implied by the concept of one mind constitutes the nonlocal, singular implicit reality of a universal consciousness that has embedded within itself the local and explicit conscious mind of each individual. This is because universal consciousness is omnipresent; it begins at the level of the most basic quantum particles, and proceeds to produce a deeper understanding of the entire cosmos. This means that local individual research physicists, along with the electrons they are experimenting with, do not function in isolation. They both exist within the nonlocal, implicit context of a knowing universal consciousness. If particles know in advance how the experiment*

chooses to observe them, they know because universal consciousness is immanent within the researcher's mind as well as in the particles of the experiment.

During his career as a cardiologist, the Dutch scientist Pim van Lommel received many reports of near-death experiences (NDEs) from his cardiac arrest patients. These reports of NDEs from his patients happened frequently and seemed to share a lot of the same elements such as: floating up and hovering around the ceiling while they watched as the doctors and nurses worked to resuscitate their body; traveling through a tunnel where they met loved ones who told them they had to come back. Because of the large number of NDEs reported to him by his patients, he decided to study the phenomenon, which he did for more than 20 years using a large patient population. He published his findings in the medical journal *The Lancet*, which caused quite a stir among both colleagues and the lay people. Based upon his research, Lommel concluded that there is a unified field of consciousness.

This unified field of consciousness contains and connects all individual minds. It contains everything in a timeless and placeless field. The information is stored non-locally as wave functions in nonlocal space, which means that information from everywhere is contained in the field and always immediately available anywhere. Wave particles, which are responsible for storing information in the unified field, are continuously present in and around the body. The brain and body simply function as a relay station that receives information from the unified consciousness in the form of measurable and constantly changing electromagnetic fields. In the unified filed theory of consciousness, brain function can be viewed as a transceiver; the brain does not produce but rather facilitates consciousness.

This unified field of consciousness contains everything in existence including the localized minds of all individual entities, both incarnate and discarnate. It exists as an infinite field of potential, which knows no boundaries or limitations. It contains within itself every probability, from the infinitely large to the infinitely small. It comprises all things physical and those that are nonphysical. This Unified Field has also been referred to as: The Mind of God, Superconscious Mind, Universal Mind, Divine Mind, Holographic Mind, Quantum Mind, Cosmic Consciousness, and Akasha. When I consider the implications of a unified field, I am reminded of the first verse of the Shema, which is a declaration of the basic principle of Jewish belief proclaiming the absolute unity of God:

Hear, O'Israel: The LORD our God, the LORD is one.
—*Deuteronomy 6:4 NIV*

Spirit communication is possible because we are all connected in the unified field of consciousness. The mind of our higher self is the aspect of our consciousness known as the superconscious mind. It's our superconscious mind that is able to interact with the Spirit World. Connecting to and channeling this aspect of ourselves is what enables us to communicate with Spirit. You don't need guides to help you. All you truly need is to learn to connect to and work with your Higher Self (Spirit Self).

Connecting to Your Higher Self

"When you contact the Higher Self, the source of power within, you tap into a reservoir of infinite power."
—Deepak Chopra

Your Higher Self is the part of you that is connected to the Source (Creator). The Source is the ultimate creative and omniscient power of the universe. It links you to everyone and everything in the Matrix (also known as the Akasha). This universal reservoir of infinite power is always present and waiting for you to acknowledge it. Through your Higher Self you have access to this reservoir of infinite power. Establishing a connection is simply a matter of intentionally turning inward, and tuning into it. With this connection, you'll have the power to discern and communicate spirits.

Although your higher self is much greater than what you see when you look in the mirror, the following mirror exercise will allow you meet, and communicate with your higher self. During your session with your higher self, you'll have an opportunity to enter into an agreement to work together to achieve success in all your endeavors, including Spirit communication. In your mind's eye, you can seal this agreement with a handshake or by signing an agreement. Before exiting the following mirror induced hypnotic state of awareness, you'll make a post hypnotic suggestion to yourself that you will be able to access your higher self at anytime just by saying the word "unity" either out loud or in your mind.

Exercise #1

1. Set aside some time when you won't be disturbed for at least thirty minutes. You can play classical, new age or any easy listening music without words to help you relax if you want to. Also, fragrances, such as lavender can be used to contribute to a pleasant environment. Just be sure that any music you play or fragrances you use don't become a distraction. Your objective is to establish a pleasant environment and state of mind.
2. Sit comfortably in a chair facing a mirror—preferably a portable mirror that you can stand on a table in front of you. Make sure that the mirror is at eye level, and you are close enough to clearly see your eyes.
3. Now concentrate on your breathing and let the rhythm of your respirations carry you towards more calmness and stillness. Every breath in fills you with peace and every breath out releases all tension, anxiety, worry or anything else that could block your connection with your higher self.
4. As soon as you are relaxed, turn your attention to the mirror and focus on your own eyes. Gaze into your eyes and visualize your physical self merging with your spiritual self—the light being that you truly are.

5. Now simply talk to your higher self. Tell it about your concerns and your dreams. You can even ask it for advice about something you need help with. Tell your higher self that you desire to communicate with your loved ones in Spirit and you want it to work with you as your partner and guide in Spirit communication.
6. Enter a receptive mode. You do this all the time when communicating with other people. For example, when you ask someone for directions, you wait for and listen to their reply. For the most part your higher self will normally speak to you in subtle and loving ways through words, symbols, images, and feelings. (There are exceptions. For example, my higher self has broken through my conscious mind in a loud and stern voice to give me emergency instructions in a life threatening situation.) It's important to be in a receptive state of mind when receiving information from your higher self. Your higher self is always listening and is always there waiting for your invitation to receive its help.
7. Now, visualize yourself entering a written, or verbal partnership agreement with your higher self to communicate with the world of Spirit. You can seal the written partnership agreement by signing it, or your verbal agreement with a handshake. (Take the approach that resonates with you.)
8. Tell your higher self that you will say the word "unity" either out loud or in your mind whenever you desire to connect and merge your individual consciousness with the superconsciousness of your higher self.
9. Now, take a deep breath, and bring your focus back to the room. Wiggle your toes and fingers, and just sit a moment thinking about what you experienced during your session with your higher self. In the space below, feel free to write about your experience and the impressions you received.

_____
_____
_____
_____
_____
_____
_____

~ 4 ~

IS SPIRIT COMMUNICATION AN EVIL PRACTICE?

"After six days Jesus took with him Peter, James and John the brother of James, and led them up a high mountain by themselves. There he was transfigured before them. His face shone like the sun, and his clothes became as white as the light. Just then there appeared before them Moses and Elijah, talking with Jesus."

— Matthew 17:1-3 (NKJV)

A Communion of Spirits

There is a divine purpose in spirit communication. Divine purpose is both universal and personal, and defines spirit communications as a connection for the greater good. Just about every religion or faith system in the world today and throughout history, incorporates some element of belief in life after death. Many faiths and religions incorporate their beliefs abut the eternal spirit into their practices. Believe or not, Catholicism is no exception.

In 835, Pope Gregory IV proclaimed October the 31st to be observed within the Catholic Church as All Hallow's Eve, or "All Holy Evening." On this date, he decreed that Catholics everywhere were to gather and remember those who had given their lives in the name of their faith. Pope Paul VI wrote the following proclamation of the catholic faith in the June 30, 1968, *APOSTOLIC LETTER IN THE FORM OF MOTU PROPRIO OF THE SUPREME PONTIFF PAUL VI:*

> *We believe in the communion of all the faithful of Christ, those who are pilgrims on earth, the dead who are attaining their purification, and the blessed in heaven, all together forming one Church; and we believe that in this communion the merciful love of God and His saints is ever listening to our prayers, as Jesus told us: Ask and you will receive. Thus it is with faith and in hope that we look forward to the resurrection of the dead, and the life of the world to come.*

Prayer is a vital aspect of the Christian faith; however, as I stated in the last chapter, it's usually one way communication. One way communication is not what Jesus practiced. His communication with Spirit always demonstrated an immediate reply either through the voice of God, an act of God, or a discourse with dead people. According to dictionary.com, a medium is a person through whom the spirits of the dead are able to contact the living. Jesus fits this description, which means that Jesus was also a medium! Yes, I said it and it's true! It's recorded in Matthew 17 of the NKJV Bible, which also refers to the reincarnation of Elijah as John The Baptist (who had been slain as Jesus was just gearing up his ministry). Also, Moses and Elijah appear to be acting as guides for Jesus. The following verses taken from Matthew 17:1-9 describes Jesus's communication with the. spirits of Moses and Elijah:

> *Now after six days Jesus took Peter, James, and John his brother, led them up on a high mountain by themselves; and He was transfigured before them. His face shone like the sun, and His clothes became as white as the light. And behold, Moses and Elijah appeared to them, talking with Him. Then Peter said to Jesus, "Lord, it is good for us to be here; if You wish, let us make here three tabernacles: one for You, one for Moses, and one for Elijah."*
>
> *While he was still speaking, behold, a bright cloud overshadowed them; and suddenly a voice came out of the cloud, saying, "This is My beloved Son, in whom I am well pleased. Hear Him!" And when the disciples heard it, they fell on their faces and were greatly afraid. But Jesus came and touched them and said, "Arise, and do not be afraid." When they had lifted up their eyes, they saw no one but Jesus only.*
>
> *Now as they came down from the mountain, Jesus commanded them, saying, "Tell the vision to no one until the Son of Man is risen from the dead." And His disciples asked Him, saying, "Why then do the scribes say that Elijah must come first?" Jesus answered and said to them, "Indeed, Elijah is coming first and will restore all things. But I say to you that Elijah has come already, and they did not know him but did to him whatever they wished. Likewise the Son of Man is also about to suffer at their hands." Then the disciples understood that He spoke to them of John the Baptist.*

If communicating with the dead was okay for Jesus, it is certainly okay for me. The gift comes from the same source, God. Jesus never discouraged people from communicating with their deceased loved ones. In fact, he never mentioned mediums anywhere in the Bible, but he did encourage us to be like him.

We all have our reasons for wanting to establish and maintain communication with spirits. You might need closure; knowledge of where important papers are located; reassurance that your deceased loved one is okay; help getting through a difficult time; or a need to continue bonds with your deceased loved one through periodic communication. Regardless of the reasons, spirit communication should always be a healing experience. The first time you initiate spirit contact, you may or may not know what healing you actually need. Much of the hurt people carry with them is buried so deep within them that they are no longer consciously aware of it. Communication with Spirit should always leave you feeling inspired and hopeful.

What are Your Reasons for Spirit Contact?

Why do you want to contact Spirit? Setting an intention to communicate with spirit is the first step in contacting Spirit; however, to set your intention to obtain useful, and specific information from Spirit, you have to understand why you want to make contact. Before you initiate contact, set aside some time to really think about what you want to know, and that will help you decide what to ask.

In this exercise, you'll think about and write down your reasons for making contact with Spirit. You'll get a chance later on to apply this exercise to the activity in chapter seven.

Exercise #5

- Are you grieving the loss of a loved one? If so, who passed?

_____
_____
_____
_____
_____
_____
_____

- How long ago did they pass, and what were the circumstances surrounding their passing?

_____
_____
_____
_____
_____
_____
_____

- What unresolved issues are you experiencing in your life by the passing of your loved one?

_____
_____
_____
_____
_____
_____

- Is there specific information you need to receive from your loved one in Spirit? For example, the whereabouts of certain legal documents?

_____
_____
_____
_____
_____
_____
_____

- Did you seek the advice of your loved one in Spirit while they were alive? Are you wishing to get advice from them now that they are in Spirit?

_____
_____
_____
_____
_____
_____
_____

- Do you have a specific message to convey to your loved one in Spirit?

_____
_____
_____
_____
_____
_____

- What do you most want to know from your loved one in Spirit?

_____
_____
_____
_____

- Do you want to use spirit communication as a way to continue bonds with your loved one in Spirit? If so, what type of intentions do you see yourself setting for your interaction with them? For example, you may just want to talk to them about everything that's going on in your life without any required response from them other than feeling their presence or smelling a scent associated with their presence. In the space provided below explore the types of interactions you could possibly experience with your loved one in Spirit when you communicate with them.

The Impact of Religious Beliefs on Spirit Communication

In this section, we'll discuss the diversity of beliefs held by people regarding spirit communication, as well as the beliefs required to successfully communicate with your departed loved ones. Then we'll work on identifying any negative beliefs you might have that could interfere with your ability to communicate with Spirit.

There are many people who won't communicate with the spirit of their loved ones due to fear of the unknown; however, most fear based beliefs regarding spirit communication can be traced to negative religious beliefs. What most religious people don't realize is that the method of prayer they've been taught is a form of spirit communication where they're doing all the talking, but not listening. Many people ask God for help with issues in life; but, do they listen or follow the promptings given to them by Spirit in response to their requests? Why is it that many religious people are not aware that they are participating in spirit communication when they pray? After all, isn't God a Spirits? We are told in the New Testament of the Bible that God is Spirit, and we must worship God in spirit and truth. Most religious people have been told prayer is one way communication, and God doesn't talk back. That's just not true! Communication is a reciprocal process; it doesn't matter if you are talking to another human being or Spirit. We communicate with others to make our needs and desires known, and others communicate back to us to acknowledge and respond to our needs. People practice one way communication when they pray because they haven't been taught to receive communication through their psychic, or spiritual senses. Praying or talking to your loved ones in spirit and learning how to identify their reciprocal communication forms the crux of this book. Basically we can conclude that spirit communication is effective prayer, which occurs two ways. For prayers that request help to be effective, you must believe that your request is granted. Prayers in which you feel you must beg for help are faithless. These prayers get no results. It's the same way in spirit communication. In order to communicate with Spirit, you must believe that you can talk with your loved ones, and they can talk back. Religious beliefs can help or hinder the faith required for effective spirt communication. To determine whether or not you have the faith required for spirit communication, it becomes necessary to examine the acceptability of spirit communication based on your religious beliefs. These beliefs can be broken down into one of two main categories—authoritative and permissive.

Authoritative Beliefs

Authoritative beliefs based on religious doctrines are usually dominated by rules that are almost impossible to follow to the standard required for success. If you stray from the doctrine, then you'll surely be damned to spend eternity in hell. Authoritative religions expect its members to blindly accept and follow all the tenets of the doctrine. Questioning or challenging any of the tenets is usually not tolerated. Most authoritative religions do not believe it's acceptable for individuals to have or use psychic abilities, including mediumship, or spirit communication. Any psychic ability is thought to be the work of the devil. Even today some religious cults have gone so far as to punish or kill members they think may be possessed by the devil. Throughout the centuries, women with strong psychic abilities have been labeled witches and burned at the stake. Even to this day, witch hunts continue in some parts of the world, and women are usually the targets.

Permissive Beliefs

Permissive religions don't rule by intimidation. They recognize the individuality and gifts of each person. The reason is they accept that your gifts were given to you for a higher purpose, one that can be used to benefit society as a whole. Permissive religions have room for many different types of beliefs, as long as they work towards a positive goal. One such permissive religion is Unity. I am not endorsing Unity or any other religion, however, although Unity is purportedly a Christian based religion, it accepts many religions as being paths to God, and it does not frown upon those with spiritual or psychic gifts such as mediumship. To communicate with Spirit, you'll need to give yourself permission to do so. You can't fool your subconscious mind. Through the law of belief, you will manifest what you truly believe, including your ability to communicate with Spirit.

Fear of Evil Spirits

Possibly, you could become a victim of crime if you're not vigilant while traveling in an unfamiliar city or country. Pickpockets and scam artists abound everywhere on the planet and they are always looking for tourists who appear to be easy targets. Tourists don't stop traveling for fear they might be victimized by unsavory individuals seeking to rob them; and mediums don't stop communicating with spirits for fear that unsavory entities might try to harm them. Just as there are precautions you can take to feel safe while traveling, there are precautions you can take to feel safe while communicating with spirits. There is no reason to fear traveling, nor is there any reason to fear spirit communication.

An individual's beliefs and expectations about the safety of communicating with spirits is often intertwined with his or her fundamental religious beliefs. Many people fear they will encounter an evil spirit if they attempt spirit communication. You create your reality through your thoughts, and beliefs, so if you expect strongly enough that you will encounter an evil entity while trying to communicate with your deceased loved one, then you could conceivably manufacture such an entity. We are all very powerful beings. Whatever you're focusing on, you're going to attract more of it. The spirit world is very thought responsive, and an extremely negative frame of mind can result in experiences that will only serve to reinforce your negative thoughts. If you think to yourself: *I'm vulnerable, there are demons everywhere, and the devil is out to get me,* then you're actually asking the Creator (God) to bring you those experiences. Through your negative expectations, you're going to manifest whatever negative thoughts you believe. So, if you believe you're going to be harmed by a spirit, you're already setting yourself up for the experience. Through positive faith in the goodness, and protection of the Great Spirit (God/Creator) you can transmute negative beliefs into positive ones. There is nothing to fear, but fear, when communicating with loved ones in Spirit. It's really about knowing that you're in charge of your experience. You take charge of your experience by believing that sprit communication is safe and you are protected, and also by setting your intention (expectation) to have a loving connection with your deceased loved one.

Unbelievers in Spirit Communication

Simply stated, an unbeliever is—for whatever reason—a doubter or skeptic in something that others may believe in. Some people would jump at the chance to communicate with their deceased loved ones, but they don't believe that it's possible. Atheists refuse to believe in a God or life after death, no matter how convincing an argument you present to them. Agnostics on the other hand, don't completely deny the possibility of God or life after death; they just believe that it's impossible to know whether or not God really exists. Among the unbelievers are people who believe there's a God, and that their loved one is in heaven, but they don't believe in the validity of spirit communication.

Belief is the key that opens the door to the seemingly impossible. Belief is an incredibly powerful state of mind. Your belief system not only defines and shapes who you are, but it also determines your potential. Henry Ford was spot on when he said, "Whether you think you can or think you can't - you are right." Even atheists have experienced communication with a deceased loved one during EMDR (Eye Movement Desensitization and Reprocessing) therapy, obviously not because they believed in spirit communication or religion, but because they trusted and believed in the therapy they were receiving, which allowed their therapist to put them into the receptive state of consciousness necessary for spirt communication to occur. In other words, even atheists have experienced after death communication during EMDR, even when the goal of therapy was to address their trauma, and not to induce after death communication.

Current research shows that our expectations influence our perception of everything we experience, from how we enjoy a particular activity to how we perform on certain tasks. Whether we do so consciously or not, we form expectations about things. These expectations may be based on what we are told by others or by the subconscious beliefs we hold. How well we expect to perform in certain activities greatly influences the outcome of our performance. High expectations seem to improve performance while low expectations seem to undermine performance. Sometimes, to succeed in a new activity, we must change our expectations. We accomplish this by replacing restrictive beliefs that no longer serve us with permissive ones that will allow us to succeed. In a nutshell, if you want to succeed in spirit communication, you'll have to replace restrictive beliefs that negatively influence your expectations, with permissive ones, which will positively influence your expectations. In the exercises that follow, you'll explore your beliefs about Spirit Communication, which will help you identify and replace any negative ones with positive ones.

EXERCISE #1

Identifying Beliefs About Sprit Communication

- Do you pray? Do you believe in the efficacy of prayer? Regardless whether the answer is yes or no to either question, please explain why.

- Do you believe in one God or many gods? Do you believe deity hears you when you pray? If so, why?

- Do you believe in praying to angels? If so, why?

- Do you believe in praying to the saints or other deities? If so, why?

- Do you believe in divine signs? Was there ever a time when you asked the God of your understanding, angels, saints, or other deities for a sign, and got it? If yes, then please briefly explain.

- Do you sometimes believe you might accidentally contact something evil while praying to God, the angels, saints, or other deities? If yes, then please briefly explain why. If not, then speculate on why you've never experienced fear while praying. Was it because you had set your intention to talk to God? How might setting your intention to talk to God apply to setting your intention to talk to your loved ones in heaven? Reflect and write down your thoughts and feelings.

EXERCISE #2

Identifying Your Beliefs About Good and Evil

- Briefly describe your beliefs about good and evil.

- Do you believe there are evil forces out there that you should worry about? If yes, then please briefly explain.

- Do you believe the forces of good are greater than any forces of evil? If yes, then please briefly explain why.

  _____
  _____
  _____
  _____
  _____
  _____
  _____

- Do you believe you have the personal power to overcome the hurtful actions and intentions of mean spirited people? If yes, then briefly identify and explain the strengths you draw upon to deal with their negative behaviors. How might your personal power in the physical realm carry over into the spiritual realm so that you feel safe?

  _____
  _____
  _____
  _____
  _____
  _____
  _____

- Do you believe you have a guardian angel, or loved one in Spirit who watches over you to guide and protect? If so, take a moment to acknowledge them and feel their presence. Briefly explain how their presence makes you feel.

  _____
  _____
  _____
  _____
  _____
  _____
  _____

- Are your religious beliefs permissive or restrictive? If you have restrictive religious beliefs, how do you feel in your heart about communicating with your loved ones in heaven? Is it good or evil? Keep in mind that we pray to God, angels, saints, and other deities. If it's okay to talk to divine beings in heaven, why would it be wrong to talk to our loved ones who are also in heaven? Take a few minutes to reflect on these questions and write down your thoughts and feelings.

_____
_____
_____
_____
_____
_____
_____

- Do you believe you'll encounter an evil spirit if you attempt to communicate with your loved ones in heaven? If so, what beliefs are creating this fear? What actions do you believe you could take to empower yourself and feel safe during spirit communication?

_____
_____
_____
_____
_____
_____
_____

- How might your beliefs about good and evil interfere with your efforts to communicate with your loved ones in Spirit?

_____
_____
_____
_____
_____
_____
_____

Exercise #3

Identifying Your Beliefs About the Validity of Sprit Communication

- Have you ever been to a psychic medium for a reading? Did you feel like they were actually in touch with your loved one? Did you feel that the medium attempted to fish for information by asking a lot of questions? Did they use a form of divination such as Tarot Cards, or Runes to attempt to get information from a spirit? If they did, they were not an authentic psychic medium. An authentic psychic medium is able to see, hear, feel and communicate with spirits on every level by using their psychic faculties. They don't need, or use tools associated with divination. They are able to give you evidential information upfront without asking questions. They often begin their message by using phrases such as *I feel, I see, or I hear*. They leave it to you to identify the spirit coming through; they won't try to interpret the message either. Describe any experience you've had with a medium. Did you believe they were authentic? If you've never been to a psychic medium, do you believe in the existence of authentic ones?

- Have you ever used a spirit board such as the Ouija to attempt spirit communication? I personally don't condone the use of a spirit board as a game. People who dabble in spirit communication or fail to use the right intent are setting themselves up for trouble. Would you open the doors to your house and let just anyone in? I think not! People who know how to use the Ouija correctly as a tool with the right intent don't usually encounter problems; however, there is a better way to communicate with Spirit, and that is to develop your psychic senses. If you have used a spirit board, describe your experience with it, if not then discuss whether or not you believe you would feel safe using one.

- Do you believe you've received a message from a loved one in Spirit during a dream? These are known as dream visitations. If you think you may have had one, what characteristics of the dream made it feel like they really visited you? If you've never had a dream visitation, do you believe it's possible?

_____
_____
_____
_____
_____
_____
_____

- Do you believe you have received a sign from a loved one in Spirit? If so, describe the sign you were given. If not, do you believe it's possible?

_____
_____
_____
_____
_____
_____
_____

- Do you believe you have sensed the presence of a loved one in Spirit? If so, then briefly describe why you felt that way. If not, do you believe it's possible?

_____
_____
_____
_____
_____
_____
_____

- Was there ever a time when you believe you experienced an unexplainable fragrance associated with a loved one in Spirit? For example, if your father smoked a pipe, you might get a whiff of his favorite tobacco. If your mother wore *White Linen* perfume, then you might get a whiff of that. If your grandmother enjoyed baking fresh bread, then you may experience the smell of bread baking when there is none. This is a psychic phenomenon known as clairolfactory. If you believe you have experienced clairolfactory, then describe it below, If not, do you believe it's possible? Describe what smell you might pick up on if a loved one was to visit you.

- Has your pet ever had an unexplainable reaction to something that wasn't there? Pets appear to be highly sensitive to spirits, and often perk up when a spirit is present. Your dog might start whining or barking for no apparent reason, or may suddenly come to attention with ears perked up and tail wagging as though they were happily greeting a loved one. Cats might respond to spirits by hissing or by striking out while looking in a specific direction. Do you believe pets can see spirits? Describe any unexplainable behaviors your dog or cat may have exhibited. Also, describe any thoughts, or feelings you may have had while witnessing their behavior.

- It has been suggested that Spirits must tap into an energy source to manifest in the physical realm, and the easiest power source is electricity. Light bulbs may flicker on and off, or suddenly go out and need to be replaced frequently. Televisions, smoke detectors, or radios may frequently go on and off without a rational explanation. Interruptions in electronic equipment, especially a sudden loss of power in battery-powered equipment and devices commonly occurs when a spirit is present. For instance, Paranormal investigators find themselves having to constantly replace brand new batteries upon encountering spirits. Do you believe it's possible for spirits to use electronics to manifest or attempt communication with us? Describe any issues you've had with electronics in your home that occurred after the death of a loved one. Do you believe they were trying to get you attention?

Exercise #4

What Do You Believe About Spirit Communication?

• Based on your responses in exercise #1, what do you believe about spirit communication through prayer?

_____
_____
_____
_____
_____
_____
_____

• Based on your responses in exercise #2, what do you believe about spirit communication being good and evil?

_____
_____
_____
_____
_____
_____
_____

• Based on your responses in exercise #3, what do you believe about the validity of spirit communication?

_____
_____
_____
_____
_____

~ 5 ~

PROGRAMMING YOUR SUBCONSCIOUS BELIEFS FOR SPIRIT COMMUNICATION

"Then Jesus said to the Roman officer, 'Go back home. Because you believed, it has happened.' And the young servant was healed that same hour."
—Matthew 3:18 (New Living Translation)

"All that we are is the result of what we have thought. The mind is everything. What we think we become."
—Buddha

The Law of Belief

In this chapter, we'll discuss the law of belief and how you can use this law to reprogram your subconscious mind to achieve anything you desire, including the ability to communicate with loved ones in Spirit. Individuals of many different religions get, what seems like, miraculous answers to their prayers. Seeming miracles don't happen because of a particular religious creed, liturgy, ritual, ceremony, incantation, or offering, but solely because of belief or mental acceptance and receptivity of what is prayed for. Answers to prayer are the result of the individual's subconscious mind responding to the mental picture or thought in their mind. The law of your mind is the law of belief, and belief can be as simple as a thought. In the original 1903 edition of *As A Man Thinketh,* James Allen begins the book with the following statement:

> *MIND IS THE MASTER POWER THAT MOULDS AND MAKES,*
> *AND MAN IS MIND, AND EVERMORE HE TAKES*
> *THE TOOL OF THOUGHT, AND, SHAPING WHAT HE WILLS,*
> *BRINGS FORTH A THOUSAND JOYS, A THOUSAND ILLS:*
> *HE THINKS IN SECRET, AND IT COMES TO PASS:*
> *ENVIRONMENT IS BUT HIS LOOKING-GLASS.*

All your experiences, events, conditions, and acts are the reaction of your subconscious mind to your thoughts. A great way to understand how your subconscious mind works in manifesting what you believe is to think of it as a garden. As the gardener, you are constantly sowing seeds (thoughts) into the fertile ground of your subconscious mind, which will produce a harvest in your life. As I write, I am reminded of the following verse found in Galatians 6:7 of the New King James Version of the Bible:

> *Do not be deceived, God is not mocked; for whatever a man sows, that he will also reap.*

Through the Law of belief, you are constantly creating your life with your thoughts. If you have restrictive beliefs, then you will have thoughts that are limiting. If you have permissive beliefs, then you will have thoughts that are expansive. Since your beliefs (and ultimately your reality) are created and reinforced by the thoughts you think, they can be changed by thinking new thoughts. Whatever you decide to be true in your conscious mind will be impressed upon your subconscious mind. Your subconscious mind is in constant contact with the unified field (divine mind or superconscious mind). The creative energy of the divine mind molds the thoughts impressed upon it by the subconscious mind. Thoughts continuously impressed upon the superconscious mind by the subconscious mind will be projected into reality. William James, the father of American psychology, said that the power to move the world is in your subconscious mind. Henry Ford basically said the same thing, but a little differently:

> *Whether you think you can, or you think you can't--you're right.*

Austrian Psychologist Sigmund Freud viewed consciousness as having three states: id, ego, and superego (also known as the subconscious/conscious/superconscious minds). The id, or subconscious mind refers to the part of consciousness that exists just below waking consciousness. Your subconscious mind contains all of your past programming, your mental and emotional imprints from the past, your beliefs about yourself and the world around you. Your subconscious is a storehouse of all your thoughts, which releases an energetic vibration.

Through the Law of Belief (also known as The Law of Attraction) the frequency of this vibration manifests what you experience in life.

Waking consciousness, or the ego, can be defined as being alert and aware of our own thoughts, feelings, perceptions and surroundings at any given moment as we go about our activities of daily living. It creates the reality of what we perceive to be real and is central to our sense of self. Robert Collier explained the conscious mind expertly when he said:

> *It is only through your conscious mind that you can reach the subconscious. Your conscious mind is the porter at the door, the watchman at the gate. It is to the conscious mind that the subconscious looks for all its impressions.*

The superconsciousness mind, which is the mind associated with our higher self (spirit self), transcends human consciousness. It encompasses a level of awareness that sees beyond material reality and taps into the energy and consciousness behind that reality. The superconscious is where true creativity is found. Expressions of this kind of creativity are distinctive from those that come from the subconscious. The superconscious is where ideas for truly great works of art, music, prose, poetry, great scientific discoveries, and deep spiritual experiences are found. Profound healing of ailments can also take place while in this state of mind. It is through the superconscious mind that we connect with the divine mind (God/Creative Energy) and the minds of others within the cosmic consciousness (unified field).

When you begin to consistently practice attuning with your superconscious mind, you'll discover how unlimited your higher self (spirit/god self who is connected to the Godhead) really is. As you start to identify more with your higher self rather than your limited physical self, you'll discover that all kinds of limitations will spontaneously disappear from your life, and miracles will follow you wherever you go. You access the superconscious mind through your subconscious, which is the portal to higher levels of consciousness. Therefore, the process of accessing it is the same as accessing the subconscious mind, but with the intent of communicating with your higher self. I believe that being able to access the collective consciousness is what makes it possible for spirit communication to occur. It may help if you think of your individual self, or ego, as being like a separate drop of water taken from the ocean while your higher self is one with the entire ocean. Although there are perceived barriers between levels of consciousness (mind), all levels exist on a continuum without barriers; therefore, all levels of consciousness are really one.

Edgar Cayce (1877-1945) an ordinary Baptist Sunday school teacher, photographer and family man, is a prime example of an individual who mastered the ability to attune to his superconscious mind allowing him to channel his higher self. To tap into his superconscious mind, he would lie down and enter an altered state of consciousness (trance) through guided hypnosis. Then, he would access what he called The Akashic Records. The Akasha contains the collective record of all human endeavor and universal knowledge. He was also able to channel divine beings and angels while in trance. The vast scope of his readings included answering health questions; as well as questions about science, religion, history, education; and predictions about planetary and social changes. Over 14,000 of his readings are on file at the Association of Research and Enlightenment (ARE) in Virginia Beach.

Most of us have been taught to believe we are limited, and that we don't have psychic and spiritual powers. This teaching is just not true. We all have the ability to tap into the subconscious mind where we can access the psychic and spiritual powers of the superconscious mind. Remember, all levels of mind exist on a continuum without any real barriers. Whatever limitations you are experiencing are strictly due to the limiting beliefs you hold in your subconscious mind. The way to overcome them is by attuning the conscious and subconscious minds with the superconscious mind. This is accomplished by being willing to let go of your old beliefs about yourself and the world around you and reprogramming your subconscious mind with new beliefs that will allow you to access the power of your higher self who is one with Spirit (God).

Using Affirmations to Reprogram Your Beliefs

Affirmations help you gently replace the negative thoughts with positive thoughts. Every thought you think and every word you speak is an affirmation. All of our self-talk, our internal dialogue, is a stream of affirmations. You're using affirmations every moment whether you know it or not. You're affirming and creating your life experiences with your thoughts and every word you speak.

Beliefs are just habitual thinking patterns that you learned over the years. Many of them may work very well for you, but others may be limiting your ability to create the very things you want. What you want and what you believe you can have may be very different. It's important to pay attention to your thoughts so that you can begin to eliminate the ones creating the experiences you don't want, and start creating the experiences you do want.

Charles Fillmore sums this concept up perfectly with the following statement he made in his book *Prosperity: Overcoming the Thought of Lack*:

> *Whatever we bind or limit in earth, in the conscious mind, shall be bound or limited in the ideal or heavenly realm, and whatever we loose and set free in the conscious mind (earth) shall be loosed and set free in the ideal, the heavenly.*

Whatever you affirm or deny in your conscious mind determines what you experience in life. All power is given to you in heaven and in earth through your persistent thoughts. You can start changing any negative thought patterns you may have about spirit communication by using the following affirmations, or create your own.

- I am one with Divine Mind.

- Divine Spirit expresses through me as me
- I am aligned with my Higher Self.
- I am the expression of a loving God.
- I receive divine guidance in all areas of my life.
- I am pursuing an authentic relationship with Spirit (God).
- I am where Spirit (God) wants me to be.
- I'm ready to lift the veil of the spiritual realm.
- I allow for my perfect connection with Spirit to unfold with mutual love, gratitude, and respect.
- I always let love lead the way.
- I let go of fear and I'm ready to realign with my higher self and Spirit (God).
- I deepen my connection with Spirit and discover the unique ways it speaks to me.
- I am an open and clear channel to receive guidance and clarity from my higher self and Spirit (God/Source/Creator).
- Communication with spirits is a natural extension of my ability to communicate with God.
- Through love, I'm willing to learn to communicate with my Higher Self, and my loved ones in Spirit.
- Spirit (God) is always with me, guiding and protecting me.
- I am highly receptive to the information Spirit is sending.
- I am always guided to safe and positive experiences with Spirit.
- I am strengthened by my deep connection with Spirit.
- I have a close, personal and working relationship with my Higher Self and Spirit.
- I receive clear messages from Spirit and my loved one in spirit with ease.
- I have incredible powers of discernment. I know I can trust what Spirit is communicating to me.
- The Light of God surrounds me. The Love of God enfolds me. The Power of God protects me. The Presence of God watches over me. Wherever I am, God Is, and all is well!
- I am open to meeting, and channeling my Higher Self
- I am one with my Higher Self
- I feel safe opening myself up to my Higher Self
- I am opening the door for my Higher Self to connect with me

Affirmations work best if you follow a few simple rules:

1. If you're creating your own affirmations, word them positively, in the present tense. For example say, "I am confident and successful in communicating with Spirit" rather than "I will be confident and successful" which is a vague statement on a future condition, and does not compute with your subconscious mind. Also, avoid using negatively

phrased affirmations such as, "I am not a failure" because the subconscious mind does not process negations, and the phrase will be understood as "I am a failure."

2. Call up the corresponding feelings. For instance, saying ,"I am wealthy" while feeling poor only sends conflicting messages to your subconscious mind! Whatever words you're saying at the time, strive to feel the corresponding emotions of already being or having what you desire because your subconscious will be more apt to believe it. You could say, "I am in the process of becoming more attuned with my Higher Self and the spirit realm" you are not there yet, but have started the process, and it is believable.

3. Suspend established prohibitive beliefs. What we believe to be true shapes our reality. In some cases these beliefs are well-founded, but in others they're not. Or they were once accurate but are now outdated and in need of revision. What researchers in the fields of neuroscience and social psychology are discovering about the power of belief calls into question what is actually meant by the terms "well-founded" and "accurate." Active efforts to disprove our established beliefs can often trigger defensiveness, causing us to cling to them all the harder. But if we can sidestep the struggle over whether they're true or false, and simply suspend our established prohibitive belief in them, a whole new range of possibilities open up. Without reaching any final conclusions regarding the validity of an established negative belief, we can temporarily suspend it, and act as if we don't hold it, or as if it had no hold on us. The person who regularly suspends disbelief enters a world of possibilities—a world where the imagination is limited only by itself.

4. Repeat, repeat, repeat. Affirmations work best if you say them more than just once or twice, because you are reinforcing the message to your subconscious mind. Continue to say and meditate on your affirmation until you feel that what you are saying is true. The good thing about using affirmations is that you can fit them seamlessly into your routine.

Exercise #1

Using Affirmations to Program Your Mind for Successful Spirit Communication

Using the rules listed above, write several affirmations that will program your mind for successful spirit communication. You may use the affirmations listed above or write your own. The important things to remember in this exercise are:

- State your affirmation in positive terms;
- Set your affirmation in the present tense;
- Say it with the corresponding feeling;
- Suspend established prohibitive beliefs.

Affirmation #1:

_____
_____
_____
_____
_____
_____
_____

Affirmation #2:

_____
_____
_____
_____
_____
_____
_____

Affirmation #3:

_____
_____
_____
_____
_____
_____
_____

Reprogram Your Beliefs by Visualizing Successful Spirit Communication

Visualization is the process of using concentrated thought power to consciously manifest your desires—any desire. It is a technique that allows you to relax, imagine, feel, and believe that what you create in your inner world will manifest in your outer world. Through visualization you change your outer world by changing your inner world. And the best approach is to assume a child-like sense of wonder. Let go of everything you have been taught to believe is possible, and learn to imagine your wish fulfilled.

Your subconscious mind understands and responds extremely well to pictures. It's such a powerful tool, it can be used to manifest your ability to communicate with Spirit. Start by getting in a comfortable position, either sitting or lying down in a quiet place where you won't be disturbed or distracted. Completely relax you whole body, starting from your the top of your head and moving down to your toes. Breathe slowly and deeply while counting from ten to one, feeling yourself getting more deeply relaxed with each count. Once you have relaxed, start to imagine yourself safely and confidently communicating with your loved ones in Spirit. Continue the visualization for a long as you find it sustainable or enjoyable, which could be as long as one to ten minutes per session, or longer.

If doubts or contradictory thoughts arise, don't try to resist them, just let them flow through your consciousness, and return to a feeling of knowing that your subconscious mind has the creative power of the Universe to manifest your desires according to your demands. To boost the power of visualization even further, be sure to emit strong, positive emotions while you picture these wonderful things in your mind. Allow feelings of love, gratitude, peace, and joy to flow through you as if you were truly having these experiences.

It's okay to bring your mental picture to mind throughout the day, knowing that your visualization has been created by the subconscious mind in the astral realm and is in the process of being manifested into physical reality. Make strong positive statements to yourself that it is now coming to you. See yourself receiving it or achieving it.

When you reprogram your subconscious mind, new opportunities and urges will appear in your life. For example, a friend that you haven't heard from in a long time may call and ask you to attend a Spiritualist church service or development circle with her. This activity is definitely related to your desire to communicate with a loved one in spirit and provides you with an opportunity to receive either a message from a loved one, or to develop your ability to communicate with Spirit directly, or both. It's important that you act on opportunities and urges that will allow your ability to communicate with Spirit to materialize.

Exercise #2

Reprogram Your Beliefs by Visualizing Successful Spirit Communication

In the exercise below, you will complete the six steps of creative visualization for successful spirit communication, and then write about your experience identifying any areas of difficulty you may have experienced with the process. For example, you might not be a visual person so visualization may be difficult for you. If this is the case, you can modify the exercise by replacing the visualization component with an auditory or feeling component. The important concept here is that you perceive the end result is accomplished, and that you have been granted your desire to effectively have a two way conversation with Spirit.

The Six Steps of Creative Visualization

Step #1: Relaxing The Body & Mind Through Diaphragmatic Breathing
The first step in creative visualization is to relax your body and mind. Relaxing your body and mind allows you to achieve the Alpha brainwave level, which produces the perfect state

for impressing your subconscious mind. It's my opinion that diaphragmatic breathing is the perfect technique for achieving relaxation to prepare you for your creative visualization session. You can perform this creative visualization either sitting up or lying down.

To perform this exercise while sitting in a chair:

- Sit comfortably with your feet on the floor, and avoid slouching. Make sure your shoulders, head and neck are relaxed.
- Place one hand on your upper chest and the other just below your rib cage. This will allow you to feel your diaphragm move as you breathe.
- Breathe in slowly through your nose so that your stomach moves out against your hand. The hand on your chest should remain as still as possible.
- Tighten your stomach muscles, letting them fall inward as you exhale through pursed lips. The hand on your upper chest must remain as still as possible.

To perform this exercise while lying down:

- Lie on your back on a flat surface (or in bed) with your knees bent. You can use a pillow under your head and your knees for support, if that's more comfortable.
- Place one hand on your upper chest and the other on your belly, just below your rib cage.
- Breathe in slowly through your nose, letting the air in deeply, towards your lower belly. The hand on your chest should remain still, while the one on your belly should rise.
- Tighten your abdominal muscles and let them fall inward as you exhale through pursed lips. The hand on your belly should move down to its original position.

Diaphragmatic breathing, also called abdominal, or belly breathing encourages full oxygen exchange — that is, the beneficial trade of incoming oxygen for outgoing carbon dioxide. This type of breathing slows the heartbeat and can lower the blood pressure. Current research studies show that deep diaphragmatic breathing exercises stimulate the vagus nerve, which activates the parasympathetic nervous system thereby producing a relaxing effect on the body and mind.

Step #2: Merge With Your Higher Self & Connect With Creative Power

The second step in the creative visualization process is to merge with your higher self, which will allow you to connect with the creative force of the universe. You share creative power with every manifestation of energy that exists, and you have the right to use this power. In the exercise in chapter three, you made a post hypnotic suggestion to say the word "unity" (either out loud or in your mind) whenever you desire to merge your individual consciousness with the superconsciousness of your higher self. When you merge with your higher self, you have the ability to become one with everything and everyone in the universe, thereby losing all conscious thought of separateness. Your higher self—the god/goddess within you—has a direct link to the Creator of the universe, and automatically knows how to connect with creative power. Connect with this power now by saying the word "unity."

Step #3: Visualize Yourself Having a Two Way Conversation With Spirit

The third step in the creative visualization process is to use the power of your imagination to conceive the form. Now, imagine yourself going into a movie theater. You sit in the center seat with the best view of the screen. The lights go dim, and the movie begins. On this movie screen imagine a scene where you are sitting on a park bench in the middle of a beautiful garden. The air is filled with the perfume of all the fragrant flowers, shrubs, and trees that surround you. You look up, and in the distance you notice the figure of someone walking towards you on a beautiful flagstone path. As this person gets closer, you recognize that it is actually a loved one you have been wanting to talk to. You feel yourself becoming more and more excited as they approach you with a big loving smile on their face. You smile back, your heart full of joy and excitement at prospect of seeing them. You stand up and run towards them, colliding with them in a loving embrace. You walk arm in arm back to the bench where you sit down together and start a conversation. In this two way conversation, you can clearly hear and understand every word they say in response to your communication. Before parting, you both agree to meet periodically in the garden where you can catch up on things. Allow yourself to feel the joy, and excitement of meeting and communicating with your loved ones in Spirit anytime you desire to.

Step #4: Know Beyond a Shadow of a Doubt That This Will Be Done

The fourth step in creative visualization is to accept success. You must want it and welcome it. Your creative seed is planted in the astral realm and you are now expecting it to manifest in the physical realm. Believing that you have received your vision isn't wishful thinking or lying to yourself. It is a metaphysical concept that can be found in the Bible. Mark 11:24 in the KJV Bible states:

> *What things soever you ask for when you pray, believe that you receive them, and you shall have them.*

Matthew 21:22 states it a little differently:

And all things, whatsoever ye shall ask in prayer, believing, ye shall receive.

Believing that you have received is about having the kind of expectant faith, or knowing, that is "the substance of things hoped for, the evidence of things not seen" as written in Hebrews 11:1 (KJV). You must know beyond a shadow of a doubt that what you have created in your visualization will be done for you!

Step #5: Take Inspired or Compelled Action

The fifth and final step for creative visualization is taking action when you feel inspired or compelled to do so. You cannot have a two way conversation with Spirit unless you take the steps to learn how to achieve an alpha or theta state of consciousness.

Exercise #3

In the space provided below, describe your experience with the visualization process.

_____
_____
_____
_____
_____
_____
_____
_____
_____
_____
_____
_____
_____
_____
_____
_____
_____
_____
_____

~ 6 ~

TYPES OF AFTER DEATH COMMUNICATION

"Bidden or unbidden, God [Spirit] is present."
—Desiderius Erasmus Roterodamus

Spontaneous After Death Communication

Just as your family and friends in the physical realm occasionally stop by to visit, the spirits of loved ones also stop by occasionally for a visit. This visit might occur when you're involved in an activity that you enjoyed together while your loved one was alive, or when you need comfort and encouragement.

There are five main categories of ADCs: spontaneous, facilitated, assisted, requested, and self-induced. Spontaneous After Death Communication (sADC) is the unexpected, or uninvited experiences of contact or communication with the deceased is the most common type of After Death Communication (ADC) experienced by the bereaved. Spontaneous ADC has received a lot of attention from researchers who have referred to the phenomenon as grief apparitions, afterlife encounters, post-death encounters, post-death contact, extraordinary experiences, ideonecrophic experiences, and reunion experiences. Common types of sADCs experienced by the bereaved include, but are not limited to, the following phenomena:

- sensing the presence of the deceased;
- visual (seeing an apparition or having visions);
- olfactory (smell);
- tactile (touch);
- auditory (hearing voices or sounds);
- powerful dreams;
- hearing meaningfully timed songs on the radio or music associated with the deceased;

- messages from objects (missing object or lost object found);
- communication through electronic devices (flickering lights, t.v. shutting on and off; smoke alarm coming on when there's no smoke, etc.);
- pet behavior (appear has if they are interacting with an invisible person);
- natural phenomena including unusual behavior from butterflies (landing on your shoulder or hand) birds (especially cardinals pecking on glass to get your attention)

Spontaneous After Death Communications are universal in nature because they occur in all socioeconomic and religious groups, all types of death, and at various times after the death. Although they may vary in intensity and impact, sADCs are a common, natural and normal part of the grieving process.

Facilitated After Death Communication

After death communication that occurs while using a protocol under the direction of a trained facilitator is termed facilitated after-death communication (fADCs). There are three main types of fADCs: psychomanteum, EMDR, and hypnotic-induced. It's important to note here that these methods can also be self-induced.

Psychomanteum fADCs

The first well-documented method for the facilitated induction of after-death experiences was developed by Raymond Moody in 1992. He called this method a psychomanteum. The concept of the psychomanteum is based on ancient oracle rituals and involves a mirror gazing procedure in a reduced sensory environment. The psychomanteum process involves spending time in a quiet, dimly lit room or booth. At one end is a tilted mirror. The participant softly gazes at the darkness reflected in the mirror with the intent of contacting a deceased individual. This psychomanteum creates an environment which allows the subconscious mind to flourish.

The facilitator guides the participant through the process by creating a safe atmosphere for the participant to share personal thoughts and feelings. To promote a positive experience, individuals wishing to use a psychomanteum to connect with the deceased may benefit from choosing a trained facilitator.

Individuals who participate in psychomanteum sessions report a variety of experiences similar to the content of sADCs. These include a sense of presence, physical sensations, external phenomena in the room, imagery that appears in the mirror, and dialogue; as well as auditory, visual, and olfactory phenomena.

EMDR fADCs

Eye-movement desensitization and reprocessing (EMDR) is a standard psychotherapeutic technique that uses visual, auditory, or kinesthetic bilateral stimulation that rhythmically stimulates both sides of the body to induce a state of consciousness that allows for psychological reprocessing. While using EMDR in the clinical treatment of patients with post-traumatic stress disorder, Psychotherapist Allan L. Botkin, PhD noticed that many of his patients were reporting sADCs. He discovered that a particular sequence of psychotherapeutic events could be used to deliberately induce the phenomena. Botkin termed his approach "induced after-death communication" or "IADC®.".In the first 83 patients for whom Botkin attempted to induce ADC, 81 (98%) achieved an ADC experience. He considered a successful ADC experience as being any perceived sensory contact with the deceased.

Hypnosis fADCs

A hypnotic trance state is a waking state of conscious awareness in which an individual's attention is detached from his or her immediate surroundings and directed inward. In hypnotic fADCs, a trained hypnotist or hypnotherapist induces a state of intense focus or concentration (trance state) in the individual being hypnotized. This is a guided process with verbal cues and repetition. By the use of suggestions, the hypnotist is able to guide a willing individual into a state of trance. (An individual must be willing because no one can hypnotize you against your will.)

Everyday trance states are part of our common human experience, such as getting lost in a good book, driving down a familiar stretch of road with no conscious recollection, while in meditation or prayer, or when undertaking a monotonous or a creative activity. Conscious awareness of our surroundings versus our inner awareness is on a continuum; therefore, when we are in these states, our focus is predominantly internal, but we do not necessarily lose all outer awareness.

Entering a hypnotic trance state enables an individual to bypass the critical mind of the ego (waking conscious state) which interferes with his/her ability to make contact and communicate directly with the spirit realm, including their higher self. I'll discuss more about trance states later on in the chapter.

Assisted After Death Communication

While it is possible for anyone to experience communication from the deceased, a medium is someone who has this experience regularly, reliably, and often on-demand. It has been said that all mediums are psychics but not all psychics are mediums. A psychic is someone who receives information from their higher-self about or from living people, distant locations or events, and/or times in the future or in the past that they have had no prior knowledge of. A medium is someone who is psychic, but can also perceive and receive information from spirits. Mediums are sometimes called psychic mediums or spiritual mediums, depending upon whether they are a natural medium or medium who practices as part of a Spiritualist Church. I refer to myself as a psychic medium because my abilities have been a natural aspect of me all of my life, and I am not a member of a spiritualist church.

Researchers have validated the ability of mediums to report accurate and specific information about the deceased under controlled laboratory conditions. During a mediumship reading, the medium shares messages received from Spirit with *sitters*—friends or relatives of the deceased—who wish to receive these messages. The sitters receiving messages conveyed by the medium are having what is called an assisted after-death communication experience.

Previous quantitative research has shown that mediumistic experiences appear to involve receiving rather than retrieving information. The mediums observed emphasized that they can't call up a particular spirit to order; however, a receptive medium may well be contacted by the relevant spirit. Therefore, in order to create accurate expectations prior to readings, sitters should remember that mediums are not able to control exactly who communicates or what information is reported during readings. Many mediums will convey this fact prior to readings in order to give their sitters realistic expectations. Mediums usually report three types of information during readings:

- evidential information that identifies characteristics of the deceased,
- information about events in the sitter's life that have occurred since the death,
- and specific messages for the sitters.

Evidential information helps the sitter verify that the information reported by the medium is coming from his/her loved one. This information can include physical attributes such as hair and eye color, height, build, tattoos, age, name, home, occupation, cause of death; unique scars or birthmarks; style of clothing worn while alive; personality traits; favorite foods; events, and places; as well as relationships with other deceased people or animals with him/her,

Information about events in the sitter's life since the death provide evidence that the deceased continue to observe and participate in their lives. A medium may say things like, "He likes your new car," "She saw the painting you made," "He was there walking you down the aisle," "She's happy you named the new baby after her," or, "I'm the white mist you saw in the baby's room last month. I watch over her and the whole family."

The third type of information mediums report involves messages specifically for the sitters. These may include simple messages such as "I love you" to messages intended to alleviate guilt or sorrow such as "There was nothing you could have done to prevent my death," or "My death was not your fault," or "It was time for me to go." Messages can also offer advice such as "Now is a good time to sell your house." They might reprimand you, I.e., "Why hasn't my headstone been installed yet?" Sometimes they just want to give you encouragement such as, "It's time to start dating again." Other specific messages they may want to give are: "I'm ok," "I'm still with you," "I'm not suffering or in pain," "Please forgive me," or "I forgive you," and "Please don't have any regrets." The information reported by mediums during aADC allows sitters to recognize that their relationship with the deceased still exist and assures them of their continuing bonds.

Requested ADCs

Requested after-death communication (rADCs) refers to communication with the deceased that occurs as a result of the initiator inviting the deceased to communicate by using physical apparatuses, such as a ouija board, or technological apparatuses such as voice recorders, or spirit boxes. Examples of rADCs Tools:

- Ouija Boards
- Spirit Boxes
- Digital Recording Devices
- Binary Response Device s— Yes/No Boxes
- Spirit Box Apps — downloadable to cell phones (apple & android)

I don't condone the use of such apparatuses to communicate with spirit because they are often misused through ignorance as a hobby, or game. Communication with Spirit is a serious undertaking and should not be approached as a frivolous activity for ghost hunting enthusiasts. These apparatuses should be used only by trained, professional individuals with a serious need to communicate with Spirit, such as adding to the body of legitimate university or paranormal research/study efforts, or in helping to validate a haunting in order to cross a spirit over, or perform a cleansing.

Self Induced After Death Communication

Self induced ADC is achieved by implementing a method to bring about an altered state of consciousness known as Trance. Before I can explain what Trance is, you'll need to understand what brainwaves are and how they influence consciousness. A brainwave is a measurable and recognizable pattern of electrical impulses the brain. There are five waves that have been identified in the human brain: beta, alpha, theta, delta, and gamma. Each brainwave has its own frequency, which is measured in cycles per second, known as Hertz (Hz). Each frequency has its own set of characteristics, which represents a specific level of brain activity, and a unique state of consciousness. As you can see from the diagram on the next page, brainwaves increase in frequency from lower to higher states consciousness. Higher brain waves are dominant when we are engaged in critical thinking, are hyper-alert, experiencing anxiety, having nightmares and displaying impulsive behavior. Lower brainwaves are dominant when we feel sluggish, inattentive, scattered, or depressed.

**Gamma Wave
(38-42 Hz)**

- Intense Concentration
- Problem Solving
- High-level information processing,

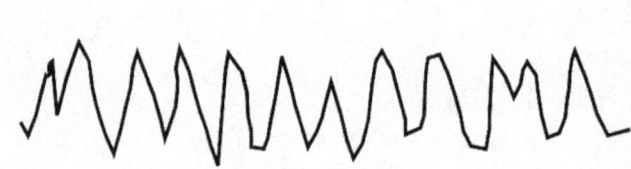

**Beta Wave
(12-38 Hz)**

- Physically Active
- External Focused
- Task Oriented
- Active Conversation

**Alpha Wave
(8-12 Hz)**

- Meditation
- Relaxed
- Focused
- Receptive Attention
- Intuitive
- Not Drowsy
- Deep Alpha is a Good wave for Psychic & Mediumship Work

**Theta Wave
(3-8 Hz.)**

- Intuitive
- Creative,
- Day Dreaming
- Deep Meditation
- Feeling of Oneness
- Drowsy
- Light Theta is a Good Wave for Psychic & Mediumship Work

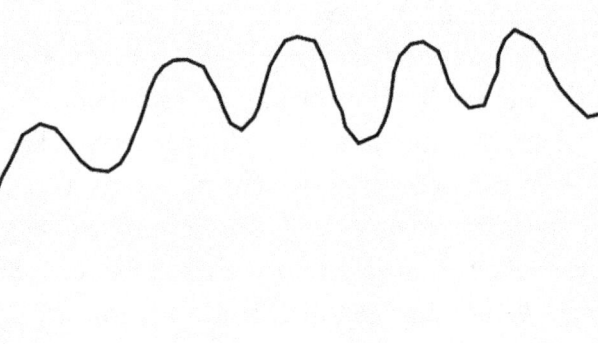

**Delta Wave
(0.5-3 Hz)**

- Deep Sleep
- REM Sleep
- Dreaming

Five Brainwaves
Shirley Smolko

- Gamma (above 40 Hz) is the insight wave, and also the fastest frequency at above 40 Hz. Very little is known about this state of consciousness, however initial research shows Gamma brain waves are associated with bursts of insight and high-level information processing.
- Beta (14-40Hz) is the frequency associated with normal waking consciousness. It is a heightened state of alertness, logic and critical reasoning, but can also translate into stress, anxiety, fear, and restlessness. This is the level of consciousness we are in when we are physically active.
- Alpha (7.5-14 Hz) is the frequency present in deep physical and mental relaxation, and can occur just by fixating or closing the eyes, during a daydream, or in light meditation. It is the optimal time to program the mind for success and it also heightens your imagination, visualization, memory, learning and concentration. It is the gateway to your subconscious mind, and the voice of your intuition, which becomes clearer and more profound the closer you get to 7.5 Hertz.
- Theta (4-7.5Hz) waves are present during deep hypnosis, deep meditation and light sleep, including the all-important REM dream state. It is the realm of your subconsciousness.
- Delta (0.5-4Hz) is the deep sleep wave. It is the slowest of the frequencies and is experienced in deep, dreamless sleep. This level of deep sleep is important for the healing process as it is linked with deep healing and regeneration.

Alpha brain waves are considered the bridge between the conscious mind (beta or gamma brain waves) and the subconscious mind (theta or delta brain waves). People who experience a light trance are in an alpha brain wave state. People who go into a deep trance are in a theta brain wave state. The subconscious mind is accessible in the alpha brainwave state and dominant in a theta brain wave state. Being in either brainwave will allow you to access the subconscious mind; however, you may not remember the communication that comes through while in deep theta trance states.

A trance state is an altered form of consciousness in which a person is neither fully awake nor fully asleep. During ADC, the conscious mind is present and watching, while the subconscious mind is providing information from Spirit. Trance states are sometimes referred to as "zoning out." In general, trance is a temporary marked dominance of either the sympathetic or parasympathetic branch of the autonomic nervous system. Sympathetic trances are characteristic of the trance states caused by shock, excitement, chaos, fight or flight reactions to trauma, panic states, and the agitation associated with psychotic states. An increase in heart rate, blood pressure and respiration are the hallmarks of this type of trance.

Parasympathetic trances are characteristic of the soothing, calm states, associated with therapeutic hypnosis and meditation. Lower blood pressure and slower, more even respirations are the hallmarks of parasympathetic trances. This is the trance state we need to induce in order to initiate after death communication, and is achieved by changing brain wave activity from a faster frequency to a slower one such the alpha or theta level. These two brainwave frequencies allow you to remain awake while focusing your attention inward, so that you can consciously process the information you are receiving from the subconscious mind; however, you may feel very drowsy while in the theta frequency range.

Self-Induced Hypnotic Trance

The trance achieved with self-induced hypnosis is no different from the trance achieved with facilitated-induced hypnosis. Both types produce the same waking state of conscious awareness in which a person's attention is detached from his or her immediate surroundings and focused inwardly. Through hypnosis you can contact your higher self, angels, guides and, deceased loved ones. Hypnosis can also be used to develop your psychic and mediumship abilities. All of us come into this world with a "sixth sense" but we usually lose the connection as we get older. As children the connection with the spirit realm is usually very strong in us, but because of religious and societal norms, we are conditioned to believe that it's our imagination, or that it's evil and we start to ignore it. By the time we reach adulthood, the connection we had with the spirit realm as children is completely severed. The good news is, hypnosis can be used to help us reconnect with our higher-self—who is connected to everything and everyone within the spirit realm.

Induction is the process used to enter a hypnotic trance. Four main elements have been identified with traditional hypnotic induction: relaxation, suggestion, expectation, and focus.

- In addition to helping highly active people to achieve focus, relaxation techniques may also help deepen an individual's trance level. There are different approaches to promoting relaxation, including, but not limited to breathing exercises, progressive muscle relaxation, soothing music, imagery, and meditation. The main goal of each approach is to relax the muscles so that an individual may focus the mind without bodily distraction.
- Suggestion is necessary in directing the mind toward a specific goal. Hypnosis uses the powerful effects of attention and suggestion to produce a broad range of subjectively compelling experiences and behaviors. For more than a century, clinical hypnotic suggestion has been used successfully as an adjunct procedure to treat a wide range of medical conditions.
- Expectation is the sole determinant of hypnotic responses. Based on the Response Expectancy Theory, what people experience during hypnosis depends on what they expect to experience. This theory is supported by research showing that both subjective and physiological responses to hypnosis (including placebos) can be altered by changing someones expectations.
- Of all the four elements, focus is the only one that is truly required for producing a successful hypnotic induction. Even when all of the other elements are present, without

focus it's impossible to induce hypnosis. Once focus is obtained, the doorway to the spirit realm through the subconscious mind is opened and sustained for as long as the focus is maintained.

Hypnosis is the focusing of the conscious attention within a narrow corridor of influence. The conscious mind tells us that blue is blue and if it receives a suggestion that it is red, it will intervene to ensure that the correct perception is formed. This is known as the critical factor of the conscious mind. When we access the subconscious mind through trance, the critical factor is circumvented and we will accept that blue is red without objection. The reason hypnosis is so useful is because it allows the subconscious mind to be accessed and influenced through suggestion. Hypnosis is a wonderful tool for accomplishing spirit communication in addition to any other goals you may have. However, traditional hypnotic techniques can be long, drawn-out procedures that are just not necessary for achieving a focused, receptive mode of consciousness, nor is it necessary to have someone else hypnotize you. You can quickly and easily induce trance in yourself. In order to simplify the self hypnotic process for spirit communication, I have created my own technique called Rapid Induction Spirit Communication Hypnosis or RISCH™, which I cover in the next chapter.

Exercise #1

Have you experienced any of the types of ADCs noted above? If you have, please write about it in the space provided below.

_____
_____
_____
_____
_____
_____
_____
_____
_____
_____
_____
_____
_____
_____

~ 7 ~

UNDERSTANDING THE LANGUAGE OF SPIRIT

"During the past fifteen years, I have been frequently surprised, and sometimes awed, by the numerous ADC encounters involving deceased loved ones. Clients, students, and colleagues have shared their grief with me, and often their unusual stories as well. I have found that their ADC experiences engaged the senses of sight, hearing, touch, and smell as well as the intuitive faculties, sometimes referred to as our sixth sense."
—Louis E. LaGrand, Ph.D.

The Clairs

Current parapsychological theory holds that the consciousness of ghost exists as pure energy and is able to communicate telepathically with the living through extrasensory perceptions. In this chapter, you'll learn how to communicate in a new language—the language of Spirit. This language is telepathic in nature because spirits communicate by thought transference. Communication from one mind to another incorporates many different modes of extrasensory perception. These modes of perception are known as the *Clairs*. The following Clairs can be used by spirits to communicate with the living:

- clairvoyance (clear seeing),
- clairaudience (clear hearing),
- clairempathy (clear emotion),
- clairsentience (clear feeling),
- clairgustance (clear tasting),
- clairolfactory (clear smelling), and
- claircognizance (clear knowing).

Clairvoyance

Clairvoyance, also known as second sight, is a psychic ability, which may express itself as a visual image (picture or symbol) or a vision (movie) that you see in your mind's eye. Its meaning comes from the French root *clair*, which means clear, and French word *voyant*, which means vision. Every time you dream or have a day dream you are using second sight. Clairvoyance is like having an internal television screen that displays information and pictures not readily available to your physical eyes. The region of the forehead just above and between the eyebrows is known as the brow chakra. This area is believed to be the location of the third eye. Focusing your attention on the third eye is the best way to activate psychic vision on command. You'll know you've tapped the third eye when you experience a sensation in the brow chakra area. It can feel like a touch, tingling, or tightening of the skin, or a vibration emanating from your forehead. I have always perceived this sensation as a touch and tightening of skin just above and between my eyebrows in an area about the size of a large coin—such as a US quarter.

Clairaudience

Clairaudience is the psychic sense of hearing. Its meaning comes from the pairing of the French root *Clair,* which means clear, and the Latin word *audentia,* which means hearing or listening. Spirits may use this mode of extrasensory perception to convey information to us by using sounds, words or songs with lyrics that contain the message they want to get across.

Ringing in the ears is probably one of the first signs that your clairaudient channel is open. I have experience ringing in my ears for as long as I can remember. The intensity of the ringing was so loud and distracting at times that I often complained to my mom. I can remember having a couple of hearing tests done as a child as a result of my complaining. Some mediums believe that a noticeable increase in the intensity of the ringing indicates that a spirit is nearby. Keep in mind that there are some medical conditions, such as tinnitus, that can cause ringing in the ears.

Clairempathy

Empathy, which literally translates as "in feeling," is the ability to share another being's emotions. This English word is derived from the Greek word *empatheia,* which means physical affection or passion. As you've probably already deduced, clairempathy means "clear feeling." If you have ever watched the t.v. series *Star Trek—The Next Generation*, you'll know about the ship's counsellor, *Deanna Troy*, who had the ability to strongly sense and channel the emotions of others. She is a prime example of how this ability works.

Clairempaths can walk into a room and immediately feel the emotional pain of someone present. They can also enter an environment where an argument has just taken place and sense the residual hurt and anger from that argument, as well as, sense the fear, horror, and pain of a place where a tragic event, disaster or atrocity occurred. Unless managed, the constant "influx" of emotions can have a significant detrimental impact on an empath's well-being. An experienced clairempath will tell you that it is imperative to maintain your spiritual boundaries by shielding yourself against excessive incoming energy, clearing unwanted negative energies from your auric field, and replenishing your own positive energy.

Clairsentience

By now you know that the word *Clair* means clear. Sentience comes from the Latin word *sentire*, which means "to feel." As you may have already surmised, clairsentience is *clear feeling*. There are two ways that clairsentience is experienced—external and internal. External clairsentience is the ability to feel sensations that seem to be emanating from outside the body, such as a cold spot or touch. Cold spots usually mean that there is a spirit nearby who has not crossed over. I have experienced this phenomena many times. For me, it has always meant that a spirit was trying to let me know they were there so that I would acknowledge and communicate with them. I believe spirits who have not crossed over reside in the astral realm, which is the realm of existence closest to the physical one. We are surrounded by the energy of these spirits.

Many times I have experienced the tactile sensation of walking into a large spider web. I have come to associate this experience as being in the midst of a group of spirits reaching out to me from the astral realm. On a more positive note, I have also experienced the touch of a comforting hand on my shoulder during times of emotional duress. I believe this hand is that of a deceased loved one trying to console me when I need solace.

Internal clairsentience emanates from within. During most of my mediumistic readings, a spirit will communicate to me how they died by making me feel what caused their death. For instance, someone who passed from a heart attack will make me feel pain and pressure in my chest, which radiates down my left arm. In a psychic reading, I might get information about someone's health through feeling their symptoms. I remember a scheduled phone reading I did for a lady who was terminally ill. On the morning of her reading, which was scheduled for later that afternoon, I started experiencing excruciating pain on the posterior and lateral sides of my lower ribcage that I associated with the lower lobe of my left lung. I had never read for this lady before, and as usual, I didn't ask her why she wanted the reading—I always prefer Spirit to guide the reading. When I talked to her later that day, she confirmed that she had pain in the back and side of her ribcage area that was caused by lung cancer in her left lung.

When an emotion is triggered, the brain changes what's happening in the body. For example, when you are afraid or angry, you might feel your heart start to pound and you might start breathing faster. When you are sad, you might get tears in your eyes. Emotions can also cause some muscles in your body to move automatically. For example, when you are happy you might smile, your voice might sound more excited, and you might stand up straighter. Most of the time, you might not even notice these automatic body changes. To help you recognize how this ability works, on a daily basis pay attention to any somatic emotional reactions you experience in your body. Also, pay attention to any body strain or aches that you might occasionally experience. Write about your experiences in a journal.

Clairgustance

You already know what the word *Clair* means. gustance is derived from the Latin word gustier, which means "to taste"; therefore, strung together these two words mean *clear tasting.* Clairgustance can be defined as the psychic ability to taste a substance without putting anything in one's mouth. Individuals who possess this ability are able to perceive the essence of a substance from the spiritual realm through taste.

A spirit may use this psychic faculty to convey the idea of a specific food they made often while they were alive because it was the family's favorite dish. This type of information is evidential in nature and spirits will often use evidential information to validate their identity. Spirits might also use this faculty to describe how they died. For example, I channeled a spirit who was killed by a gunshot to the abdomen. In addition to making me feel the intense heat and pain of the gunshot wound, he also made me perceive the taste of blood in my mouth. The taste had the heavy metallic essence of iron. I knew this taste well because as a child, I had to take a liquid iron supplement to treat anemia. In addition to the taste of blood, I could also smell it. In my work as a nurse, I was exposed to blood on a daily basis, and there is no denying the smell. I'll discuss more about the psychic faculty of smell in the next section.

Clairolfactory

Olfactory is derived from the Latin word *olfacere,* which means "to get the smell of"; therefore, it can be inferred that the word *clairolfactory* means "clear smelling." As illustrated by my example in the last section, clairolfactory can accompany clairgustance. It makes sense that this partnership exists on a spiritual level since our normal sense of taste and smell tend to go hand-in-hand, especially with food and drink, but this is not always be the case. Psychics often experience smells not associated with taste. For instance, I read for a lady who had lost her husband in a house fire. As soon as I started the reading, I experienced the overwhelming smell of something burning. When I told the sitter (client) that I was smelling something burning, she told me her husband had been a fireman and died when a beam fell on top of him. He had gone back into the house to try and rescue another person.

Maybe you've caught a whiff of your deceased grandmother's favorite perfume while you were cooking her favorite meal, or the smell of your deceased grandfather's cigar while you were playing golf. People frequently report smelling cologne or tobacco when there's no-one else around them and no logical explanation for where it's coming from. The smells don't usually linger; they're there long enough for you to notice them, and then they're gone.

Claircognizance

Cognizance is derived from the Latin word *cognoscere*, which means "to know"; therefore, claircognizance means "clear knowing." Have you ever known some event was going to happen without any indication why, and it did? If you have, you were experiencing claircognizance, and you wouldn't be the only one. Many people can remember instances when they just knew something was going to happen without having any proof or evidence that it would, and it did.

A good friend of mine told me about an incident of claircognizance that she experienced as a teenager. She said she attended mass one morning, and as she was taking communion, she instantly knew that she would never receive communion by this priest again because he would die. The priest died a few days later without any indication of being sick.

Exercise #1

Learning to Recognize the Clairs

Learning the "Clairs" is like learning a new language. To be able to connect and communicate, we have to learn that new language. It takes time and patience. You can't learn a new language by flying into a country, stepping off a plane, and spending an hour with native speakers. You would just be confused by the gibberish you heard. In the same way, you shouldn't expect to learn this new language of mind-to-mind communication in one session. You have to give it time. You're about to step off the plane into a new realm, and there, you'll receive thoughts, visions, feelings, words and sounds that are coming from the mind of a Spirit. Recognizing your dominant Clair(s) is the first step in determining how you will begin communicating with Spirit. Be patient, you have the innate ability to communicate with Spirit. You just have to learn how it works. This exercise will take you one week to complete. I have broken it down into seven daily segments to help make it more digestible; however, if you are feeling up to the challenge, you can tackle it all in the same day.

Recognizing Clairvoyance

Day #1:

1. Sit or lie down in a comfortable position. Close your eyes and take three deep belly breaths.
2. Relax and think of a beautiful place you have visited, maybe while on vacation, that brought you much joy (your "happy place"). Transport yourself there in your mind.
3. Visualize aspects of this place that you loved the most, such as the landscape (beach, rivers, mountains, flowers, tress) living accommodation (hotel, cottage, house) shops and restaurants.

4. Look at one aspect of this place from different angles, from each side, below, and above. For instance, if you're visualizing a coconut palm tree, look at it from each side, from underneath, and an aerial view from above.
5. Now, take three deep breaths, open your eyes, and wiggle your fingers and toes.

- If you were able to visualize your happy place, you have the ability to receive messages clairvoyantly. If not, don't worry, you'll discover your dominant Clairs. What place did you go to in your visualization? Describe what you saw with your second sight in the space provided below.

_____
_____
_____
_____
_____
_____
_____

Recognizing Clairaudience

Day #2:

1. Sit or lie down in a comfortable position. Close your eyes and take three deep belly breaths.
2. Relax and think of your favorite song. Allow yourself to hear the music in your head.
3. Listen to the chorus, which is the main part of the song that is repeated several times. (The main theme is expressed in the chorus.)
4. Pay attention to the lyrics. What are the words you're hearing?
5. Now, take three deep belly breaths, open your eyes, and wiggle your fingers and toes.

- If you were able to hear your favorite song in your head, you have the ability to receive messages clairaudiently. If not, don't worry, you'll discover your dominant Clairs. What song did you play in your head? Write down the words you heard with your second hearing in the space below.

_____
_____
_____
_____
_____
_____

Day #3

1. Sit or lie down in a comfortable position. Close your eyes and take three deep belly breaths.
2. Relax and think of an instance when you experienced a strong emotional feeling that was not related to your own mood at the time. This could have happened in any new space—upon entering a conference room, a clothing boutique, or a friend's home.
3. What mood were you in, and how did you feel prior to entering the new space?
4. How did you feel after you entered the new space? Were the new feelings congruent with your preexisting mood?
5. Now, take three deep belly breaths, open your eyes, and wiggle your fingers and toes.

The purpose of this exercise is to help you recognize your own mood and emotional feelings versus those of others. The more aware you are of your own mood and emotions, the better you will become at recognizing when you are empathing the emotions of others. In the space provided below, describe the instance of clairempathy you identified in the above exercise.

Recognizing Clairsentience

Day #4

1. Sit or lie down in a comfortable position. Close your eyes and take three deep belly breaths.
2. Relax and think of one special event in your life such as: your graduation day; the day you got married, the day you gave birth; the day you got your driver's license, or any other significant day.
3. Allow yourself to feel the emotions you experienced on the day of this significant event.
4. Pay attention to what is happening in your body while you are experiencing the emotions related to this event. Are you breathing faster? Is your heart pounding in your chest? Is your body trembling? Are you smiling? Are you experiencing any abdominal tension, or cramping?
5. Now, take three deep belly breaths, open your eyes, and wiggle your fingers and toes.

Somatic awareness of your own body on a daily basis will help make you more sensitive to somatic communication from Spirit. This exercise will help you to distinguish your own somatic feelings from those of other people or Spirit. In the space provided below, describe how the feelings you experienced in the above exercise manifested in your body.

_____
_____
_____
_____
_____
_____
_____

Recognizing Clairgustance

Day #5

1. Sit or lie down in a comfortable position. Close your eyes and take three deep belly breaths.
2. Relax and think of several of your favorite food.
3. One by one, allow yourself to experience the taste, temperature, and texture of these foods.
4. Is the taste sweet, sour, or salty? Is the temperature cold, hot, or tepid? Is there texture smooth, chunky, chewy, grainy, or bulky?
5. Now, take three deep belly breaths, open your eyes, and wiggle your fingers and toes.

- Were you able to taste your favorite foods? Did you get a sense of the temperature and texture? In the space provided below, describe your experience.

_____
_____
_____
_____
_____
_____
_____

Recognizing Clairolfaction

Day #6

1. Sit or lie down in a comfortable position. Close your eyes and take three deep belly breaths.
2. Relax and think of a time you entered a bakery, a tobacco shop, or perfume store.
3. Allow yourself to mentally smell the fragrances of those places. Focus on the scents until you are able to actually smell the them, even if it's only a whiff.
4. Now, think of a time when you smelled bread or cookies baking; smelled a cigar or cigarettes burning; or smelled the musky, flowery or citrus fragrance of perfume that no one else could smell, or that there's no reasonable rationale for.
5. Now, take three deep belly breaths, open your eyes, and wiggle your fingers and toes.

- Were you able to perceive the smells associated with the different odors? Was there one scent that was perceived stronger than the others? In the space provided below, describe your experience.

_____
_____
_____
_____
_____
_____
_____

Recognizing Claircognizance

Day #7

1. Sit or lie down in a comfortable position. Close your eyes and take three deep belly breaths.
2. Relax and think of a time you knew something without knowing how you knew.
3. Was your experience precognitive in nature? In other words, did you know something would happen before it actually did?
4. Have there been times when you just knew, without having any evidence, that someone was not being truthful with you, and later you learned that they actually did lie to you?
5. Now, take three deep belly breaths, open your eyes, and wiggle your fingers and toes.

- In the space provided below, describe those instances when you experienced Claircognizance.

_____
_____
_____

What Are Your Dominant Clairs?

- In the space provided below, write down what you believe your dominant clair abilities are.

Now that you have recognized how the Clairs are perceived, you can begin using them to communicate with Spirit. I recommend that you focus on using your dominant Clairs. For example, if you had a difficult time with the Clairvoyance exercise, but found the Clairaudient exercise to be a breeze, you may want to focus on using this mode of perception when receiving impressions. Keep in mind that it is possible to develop Clairs that you believe are dormant. If you have several dominant Clair abilities, then you may want to focus on using all of those modes of perception when receiving impressions.

There are individuals who use just one Clair to communicate telepathically with Spirit. For instance, some psychics advertise that they are *a Clairvoyant*. This is the only mode of perception they dominantly use to get information, and that's okay because they are able to get all the information they need this way; however, there are other psychics who use several dominant modes of perception in their readings, and that's okay too. Most gifted psychic mediums use several modes of perception in receiving messages from Spirit. Regardless of the modes of perception you use, use them in a way that will allow your to get complete and clear messages from Spirit.

The Symbols of Spirit

As it relates to Spirit communication, let's consider what symbols are and are not. The symbols that Spirit uses are not strange hieroglyphics, or ancient cultural icons that require special knowledge to interpret. With that said, symbols can be anything that has meaning for you or the one you are reading for (the sitter). Spirit uses your consciousness to connect with you; therefore, the symbols that you will receive most often will be personal to you. The bottom line is that Spirit will use any and all pieces of information stored in you brain to communicate with you.

Because symbols make up the primary language of Spirit we need to understand the different ways that we perceive these symbols. There are seven basic ways in which Spirits communicate using symbols:

- words,
- body language,
- emotions,
- art (pictures, objects)
- stories,
- music,
- gestures,
- numbers.

Words

Spirit will often use a word or a string of words to convey an important event, date, or concept. For example, Spirit may show you the word "May." This could represent the month of May or a sister named May. It's not your job to interpret the meaning of this symbol. Your job is to convey to your sitter what you are perceiving and allow them to make the connection with your help if it is needed.

Body Language

Many times Spirit uses body language to convey their message through posturing. I remember one instance where I was conveying a spirit message to my manicurist from her mother. My manicurist's mother showed herself to me with her arms crossed. I described to my manicurist the physical attributes of the woman I was seeing. I told her that her mother had her arms crossed, and I asked her about the significance of this posturing. She stated that her mother always stood with her arms crossed. If I had tried to translate this posturing without checking in with my manicurist first, I would have probably concluded that maybe her mother was not happy with a certain situation in the life of her daughter.

Emotions

Spirit people also communicate with us by expressing emotional energy. They use sentience to communicate the emotional content of their message to us. For example, I channeled a woman who had a very emotionally troubled life that ended in suicide. She made me feel the emotionally charged mindset she was in when she took her life so I could convey this bit of information to her niece for whom I was reading. She wanted her niece to know that she was in great emotional pain, and she wanted to end it because she was no longer able to cope. She also made me feel the remorse she had because of the hurt she had inflicted on her loved ones due to her perceived selfish act of suicide. During the debriefing of the reading, towards the end of the consultation with the sitter, I learned this spirit had been bipolar in life.

Art, Pictures, Objects

You have probably heard the saying, "one picture is worth a thousand words," this is even truer in the language of spirit. Most of us tend to think visually in terms of whole concepts with images rather than in data streams and words. With just one image an artist can capture and convey an entire mood, place, and situation. Similarly, Spirit can also capture and convey enormous amounts of information with the images they create and project into the canvas of your mind. This is probably why spirit uses the spiritual channel of Clairvoyance more than any other channel of communication. I recall a reading I did for a lady named Peggy whose best friend "Little Joe" came through during a reading. This lady attended the same Unity Church that I attended at the time. She approached me after the service and asked me if I could channel her best friend "Little Joe" who had died many years ago. I told her I would try and see if he would come through. Within a matter of seconds he came through and showed himself to me as being lean and tall. He was definitely not "Little Joe." I told Peggy what I was seeing. Little Joe wasn't little and that he was at least six feet tall. She admitted that she was trying to test me to see if I was a genuine medium, and I guess Spirit showed her that I was. Little Joe showed me that he was dressed in blue jeans and a button-down shirt with a collar. He had blonde hair and blue eyes and was very handsome. After the reading, Peggy showed me a picture of Little Joe that she had on her cell phone. It was the exact image that Little Joe had showed me during the reading.

Stories

A story can be told by something as simple as a comic strip or as complex as a movie. Spirit is good at creating plots to tell their story. For example, during one reading that I gave, the spirit of a young African-American man made contact with me. He told me his story by showing me a short movie that he projected on the screen of my mind. The following is a description of this movie:

I found myself observing a country scene that included miles and miles of rolling green fields with beautiful, stately oak trees. Each one of these trees had a yellow ribbon tied around it. Winding through the center of the field was a paid single-lane road that disappeared into the blazing orange horizon of a setting sun. I turned towards my right and saw what I perceived to be a stocky man on a Harley motorcycle. He was wearing blue jeans, a black wind jacket, black leather boots, and a black helmet. I watched as he drove his motorcycle into the sunset. I glanced across the single lane road where I saw a white wooden A-Frame house. I noticed several empty rocking chairs on the front porch. There was also a large oak tree in the front yard, which didn't have a yellow ribbon tied around it. Because there was no yellow ribbon tied around the oak tree, the man on the motorcycle drove on by the little house. I asked the Spirit what all this meant. The spirit of this man told me to ask this family to please forgive him, that he was in a good place and all was well with his soul. He said, "I am finally at peace and I want them to be at peace too."

Sounds and Music

Spirit uses sounds and music in very literal ways. For the most part even though you might not hear sounds and music from Spirit with your physical ears, you will hear them in your mind. I'm not saying that there will never be a time when you'll pick up Spirit activity with your physical ears because it does and can occur. For instance, some people experience hearing a loud bang throughout the house after the death of a loved one who has lingered around in the astral realm for a while and finally decided to crossover. I remember trying to help my extended family pack up my maternal grandmother's belongings when we heard a bang that seemed to echo throughout the house. We searched the upstairs and the front and back yards looking for the source of the noise. We found nothing. I even called the local news and weather channels as well as a local airports to inquire about any weather event or plane traffic in the area. All inquiries turned up nothing. There was definitely nothing out of place upstairs and no trees, or tree limbs falling on the house. We were not able to explain the sound. I personally receive more music communication from Spirit than sounds. The following story is just one example of how Spirit has communicated with me through music.

It was about 5:30 in the morning, and I was preparing to go to my nursing job at the hospital that day. I was applying my makeup and thinking about how the upcoming day might play out--would I have a crazy and chaotic day or would it be a calm day where my work flowed with ease. While I was having these thoughts, out of nowhere I began to hear piano and organ music. Then I heard a familiar voice singing a song. It was an old hymn that I remember hearing in church when I was a child, *Shall We Gather By The River*. I recognized the voice to be that of my great-aunt Mertie, one of my maternal grandmother's older sisters. Aunt Mertie played the organ and piano in church. As I listened to the lyrics, it didn't take much time at all for me to understand her message--that she had just passed away. I remember dropping my mascara in the bathroom sink as I ran into my bedroom to call my Grandma Nora to let her know about my visit from Aunt Mertie. As soon as my grandma answered the phone, I didn't waste any time telling her about my experience and that Aunt Mertie had passed. Her reply to me was, "I know. I got a phone call this morning letting me know that she had been rushed to the hospital where she died." We all knew Aunt Mertie had cancer several years earlier, but it had gone into remission. None of us was expecting her to die so soon. We were all caught off guard.

Gestures

Depending upon the channeling ability of the medium, some spirits will demonstrate specific mannerisms that they frequently used when alive. Sometimes a soul will compel me to exhibit a certain gesture or mannerism that they frequently displayed in life. For example, I gave a reading to the young mother of a nineteen year old gay man who had committed suicide one year earlier. He and his mother made "kissy faces" to each other on a daily basis. The first thing that I was compelled to do when I started channeling this young man was to make kissy faces to his mother. I explained to her that I was feeling compelled by the spirit that was coming through to make a gesture and that I didn't want her to be offended or take it the wrong way. When I started making kissy faces, she began to sob uncontrollably and said, "We use to make kissy faces to each other everyday." On another occasion, the father of a young lady compelled me to give this young lady a bear hug while lifting her off the floor. Fortunately for me, she was very petite. As soon as I gave her the bear hug, she knew without me saying that it was her father coming through.

Numbers

All throughout history numbers have come to mean different things to different cultures. Numbers hold value, both numerical and spiritual. The brilliant fifth century b.c. philosopher and mathematician Pythagoras believed that the world was built on the power of numbers and that everything and anything could be translated to numerical form, usually in single digits. His passion for numbers led him to travel to Egypt to study Chaldean numerology for twenty-two years.

The idea of assigning letters numerical values is known as the Pythagorean Number System and is used in modern numerology. Numerology is the relationship between a number and its mystical nature on both an individual and worldly level. Numerology is also the study of the numerical value of the alphabet. It is possible to uncover information about the world and individuals by using Numerology.

While it is beneficial to find out the universal meaning of numbers, it is imperative that you discover your personal meaning. Synchronicity, symbolism, and the meaning of numbers is all extremely personal, so be wary of prescribing a meaning to your life that may not be relevant. Instead of relying on numerology, or other universal meanings of numbers, put in a little work and explore what the numbers mean to you.

To determine what a specific number, or numbers received from Spirit means to you, try writing down every word association you have with the number. For instance, if you keep seeing the series of numbers 620, and your birthday is on June the 20th, your loved one in Spirit might be making reference to your upcoming birthday. It could be their way of acknowledging and wishing you a happy birthday. If you are planning to get married, or graduate from school on this date, then they are probably making reference to this event. This might be their way of letting you know that they are aware of the event and will be with you in Spirit. Do the numbers relate to a question you asked Spirit, such as *when is the best time to go back to college?* If so, does your interpretation stir up feelings of excitement, awe or jubilation? This is a good sign that you've found the right explanation because your body is reacting in such a heightened way. However, if the interpretation you have feels cold, flat, or detached, it's probably the wrong fit.

Exercise #2

Getting Clarity on Symbols From Spirit

1. Think of any situation in your life about which you need insight, or guidance with. Hold that situation in mind.
2. Merge with your higher self (remember, your higher self is your spirit self) by saying the word *unity.*
3. Now, ask your higher self to place a symbol into your conscious awareness that will give you the guidance you need.
4. Notice how you receive this message. Do you see it? Do you hear it? Do you feel it, or know it? What clair is your Higher self using to convey this symbol to you?
5. Now, let go of that symbol, and ask your higher self to bring you another symbol. Notice how you get this symbol. Is your higher self using the same Clair?

- What was the first symbol that came to you? What does it mean to you?

_____
_____
_____
_____
_____
_____
_____

- Describe how the first symbol came to you. Was it clairvoyance? Was it clairaudience, or clairsentience? Was it a combination of different Clairs?

_____
_____
_____
_____
_____
_____
_____

- Does your interpretation resonate with you? Does it stir up feelings of excitement, awe or jubilation, or does it feel cold, flat, or detached? Describe how your interpretation makes you feel.

_____
_____
_____
_____
_____
_____
_____
_____

- How did the second symbol come to you? Was it the same symbol or a different one? If it was a different, do you think it means the same thing as the first one? Did it help clarify the first symbol, or did it add new information to the first symbol? Please write about the second symbol in the space provided below.

_____
_____
_____
_____
_____
_____
_____
_____

The Signs of Spirit

A million different events happen in your day, and usually none of them stand out to you. When a seemingly benign event suddenly grabs your attention and makes you question if it's a sign from your loved one in spirit...it probably is. Some of the signs spirits use to let us know they are present and want to communicate with us are:

- flickering lights or frequently blown light bulbs,
- sudden changes in room temperature,
- clocks stopping,
- hearing your name called,
- feeling their presence,
- touches,
- bizarre pet behavior,

- computers,
- phones,
- speakers,
- fragrances,
- butterflies,
- dragonflies,
- birds,
- coins.

Flickering Lights or Frequently Blown Lightbulbs

Paranormal researchers believe that spirits have the ability to manipulate electricity, suggesting that flickering light-bulbs can be a sign indicating that spirits are present in your room. Some people have complained about lightbulbs blowing out despite being newly installed.

Sudden Changes in Room Temperature

Sudden drops in warmth despite door and windows being closed also signify the presence of a supernatural being. It may be experienced by everyone in the room or a particular person that the spirit might be trying to make contact with. It may be described as a cold chill through the body that can give us goosebumps when we unconsciously think of the presence of spiritual beings close by. This effect may also be stimulated by the brain, especially if your surroundings give you an eerie aura.

Hearing Your Name Called

Hearing your name being called out in your head or simply hearing noises that are inaudible to everyone else is also claimed to be a sign that loved ones from the afterlife are trying to make contact. In addition to hearing the voice of dead relatives call my name, I have also heard the voice of living relatives call my name. Without fail, I would always pick up the phone and call this living individual to discover that they were experiencing some kind of distress.

Feeling Their Presence

Feeling the presence of Spirit may be perceived as someone watching you wherever you go in the house, someone standing over your shoulder, or just in the same room with you. When this happens, it's usually because a spirit is trying to make contact with you and is unable to get your attention any other way. I have encountered this sign many times, especially in haunted houses.

A Clock Stopping

We notice a clock has stopped with the have been showing the same time for the past couple of minutes. If the time reminds you of a deceased person, perhaps the time they died, or the time you received the news of their demise, you are being visited.

Touch

Ghosts will also try to get your attention through touch, perhaps a tug on or stroking or of your hair; a touch on your shoulder; a ticklish type sensations on your face and, or body; or the sensation of walking through a spider web. Psychics suggest asking the spirit of a loved one to touch you on, say the right side of your face, to make sure that it is them rather than any unwanted force.

Bizarre Pet Behavior

If your pet begins spending an unusual amount of time in a certain area of your home or is having a reaction to something that you don't see, it is very possible they are sensing, or even interacting with a spirit. Animals can pick up on sounds, smells, and sights that are not detectable by humans. The following behaviors may be indications that your pet is sensing a spirit:

1. Your dog or cat may start tracking something that's not there. They may sit completely still, but their eyes are following something across the room. They might also get up and follow whatever they are perceiving with their nose.
2. Your dog or cat may start barking or hissing at nothing. This could mean they've heard something you haven't, but it could also mean that a spirit is present.
3. Your dog or cat may try to hide behind you out of fear or stand in front of you in an effort to protect you.
4. Your dog has rolled onto its back as if it's receiving a belly rub from an invisible hand, or they wag their tale for no reason as if someone they recognize has walked into the room. If you have a cat, they may sit up on their haunch and start pawing at nothing.

Computers

Computers turning on and off on their own, downloading documents, or sending emails that you didn't send may all be signs that a spirit is trying to contact you. The names of deceased relatives appearing on the screen have also been known to occur. A computer engineer might tell you that your computer has been infected with a virus, when actually, it has been infected by a ghost.

Phones

The day after my mother passed away, I started receiving phone calls with nothing but static on the line. These calls continued for about a week after my mother was buried. Upon doing some research, I learned that it's not uncommon for an individual to receive phone calls from a loved one who is recently deceased. The ironic thing for me is that my mother called me just to chat the night before she died unexpectedly the next morning from a heart attack. Since a phone is an electrical object, manipulating the energy to make a phone call is not much different from manipulating other electrical devices. This sign seems to be most common in the immediate days following the death.

Speakers

My husband is a golfer who happens to also love electrical gadgets. I frequently, but lovingly, refer to him as "the gadget man." Well, the gadget man bought a Bushnell blue-tooth speaker to connect to a Golf Course GPS App that he downloaded to his phone from the Apple Store. On the day of this incident, I was in the family room working on this book when the Bushnell speaker, which was plugged into a USB port and charging on the kitchen counter, started talking. At first I just ignore it because I was absorbed in my writing. I also had the t.v. on and I just couldn't hear it clearly. The Bushnell continued its chatter so I decided to turn the t.v. off and listen to it. No sooner than I turned the t.v. off, I clearly heard a female voice coming from the Bushnell; it said, "Hi, Hello." I didn't bother trying to communicate with the voice coming through because I thought that maybe my husband was playing a joke on me. I ran into the master bathroom where I found my husband just getting out of the shower, and drying off with a towel. I asked him if he was trying to pull a joke on me. He looked at me quizzically and asked me what I was talking about. I explained to him that the Bushnell had been chattering and even said hello to me. I asked him if he had been using his phone within the last thirty minutes. He said that he hadn't touched the phone in the last couple of hours. We looked at the phone log and there were no recent calls or voice messages for that day. He didn't have any devices other than his phone paired with the Bushnell Speaker.

Fragrances

One of the most common ways to identify the presence of a spirit is through scent. Fragrances associated with your deceased loved one will usually be somewhat familiar, such as a particular perfume, the smell of a favorite food—maybe apple pie—or the distinct aroma of specific brand of cigar. On the occasions my deceased mother has visited me, I have smelled her favorite perfume—*White Linen*. Because I am a medium, I have also experienced unpleasant smells associated with spirits. For example, I perceived the distinct smell of death and decay in my laundry room for which there was no explanation and my husband denied smelling (there's nothing wrong with his sense of smell). I immediately did a cleansing and removed the malodorous spirit—which I perceived to be the spirit of death—to the outside of the house.

A week later while I was at work in the hospital, our cat Sadie (who had been sick) got outside the lanai when the pool guy inadvertently left the screen door ajar. We found her about a week later, but she was clearly very sick and ran from us. We were unable to catch her, and I'm sure she died.

Butterflies

Butterflies represent the human soul in many cultures. For instance, the ancient Chinese believed that butterflies symbolized the transition of a soul from the earthly realm to the spiritual realm. The sight of butterflies after the death of a loved one has become a common sign that the soul has made its transition into the spirit world and is at peach. Some people have reported that a butterfly sat in their hand for a long period of time. Others have reported that a specific color of butterfly has followed them around for several days at a time. I have a Unity minister friend who swears that yellow butterflies followed her around for a week after her cousin died. She had helped to take care of this cousin while he was terminally ill. One of the hospice volunteers had given her cousin a quilt with yellow butterflies on it. She said she must have pulled that quilt on top of her cousin hundreds of times during his illness, and she believed he was using yellow butterflies to let her know that he is okay and thankful for the care she provided him.

Dragonflies

In addition to butterflies, some people believe that the soul of their deceased loved one has taken the form of a dragonfly to get their attention. People have reported dragonflies following them around for several days in a row while they are outdoors, and even landing and sitting on their hand. Butterflies and dragonflies symbolize two slightly different concepts. Butterflies represent endurance, hope, and transformation. Dragonflies represent wisdom, hope, comfort, and adaptability. Many people believe that the soul of their loved one shows up as a dragonfly in order to convey a message of hope, comfort, and adaptation to a new life.

Birds

When you see a Cardinal behaving oddly by hovering around, or tapping a window with its beak, this could be a message from someone in heaven. Pay attention when this happens as it could help you figure out who this message is from. Write down the date and time in your journal or on the calendar. Birds might deliver messages on birthdays of the deceased, on the day they died, or other significant holidays. You should feel relieved to know that someone in heaven is thinking about you. About three months before my late husband died, I had a Cardinal who constantly tapped on the glass panes of the French doors that opened up to the deck in the back of my house. This tapping occurred on a daily basis, and from the beginning I felt that it was my husband's mom or dad in Spirit who was trying to warn me of his impending death, which was to come unexpectedly. Unfortunately, it was a harbinger of his death. Three months after the tapping started, he died from a cerebral hemorrhage, secondary to the rupture of an AVM (Ateriovenous Malformation). An AVM is a group of blood vessels in the body that forms incorrectly. In these malformations, arteries and veins are unusually tangled and form direct connections, bypassing normal tissues. This usually happens during development before birth or shortly after. Birds have been associated as harbingers of death, but this does not normally apply on average. I believe that most of the time they are the physical embodiment of your loved ones soul. They appear to let you know they are still with you.

Coins

Coins are another widely reported possible "sign" from the departed. Many people believe that finding coins in unexpected places is a clear sign from the deceased. Some people have reported finding pennies lying on the floor, either individually or in odd groupings. They might be arranged in a circular pattern or in a line. Others have even made the claim that pennies sometimes fall out of the air to land on their heads. The reason for coins as a possible sign from departed spirits isn't completely clear. If you happen to find a coin that you think might be a sign from the deceased, it's recommended that you check the date on the coin. If the date is significant in your life, or in the life of the departed, that could be an additional sign.

If you visit cemeteries for veterans in the United States, you may see coins on the headstones. There is a meaning associated with each denomination of coin:

- **Pennies**: A penny is left on the headstone of a veteran or military member that you don't know. This is done as a sign of respect and gratitude for their service.
- **Nickels**: You would leave a nickel if you attended boot camp with the deceased.
- **Dimes**: Leaving a dime indicates that you served in the military with the deceased at some point.
- **Quarters**: Leaving a quarter on the headstone is done if you were with the deceased when they passed away.

Exercise #3

What Signs Have You Received From Spirit?

- Was there ever a time when you believed you received a sign from a loved one in Spirit? If so, write about your experience in the space provided below.

_____
_____
_____

The RISCH™ Method

Prior to initiating contact with spirits, I always say the *Unity Prayer of Protection*, not because I am afraid, but because I am cautious. In the same way I pray for protection before traveling in the physical world, I pray for protection before traveling in the spiritual world. For prayer to be effective you must believe that you have received what you requested. You can say the Unity prayer written below, or another prayer of your liking, or no prayer at all—that's up to you.

Unity Prayer of Protection

The Light of God surrounds me.
The Love of God enfolds me.
The power of God protects me.
The Presence of God watches over me.
Wherever I am, God is!
And all is well. Amen.

- Say a prayer of protection (optional).
- Find a place where you will not be disturbed for the duration of the RISCH™ session.
- Sit in a chair; rest your hands on top of your lap, and adjust yourself so that your head and neck is comfortable upon your shoulders and your body is in a comfortable position.
- You may hold a picture of your loved one or an object that belonged to them, but it is not necessary. (Pictures and objects absorb and retain the energy of the individual they are associated with. The residual energy that is left behind may give you a stronger line of communication.
- Take several deep belly breaths and feel yourself begin to relax. (Diaphragmatic breathing, aka belly breathing, was covered in chapter five.)
- Scan the room to find an object or spot on the wall that you feel comfortable visually focusing on. This focal point of interest can be the corner of a picture frame, a figurine on a shelf or just a spot on the wall. With the spot being decided, begin gazing at it as if you were looking through it. Do not divert your eyes even if they start watering

or blinking more frequently. Continue focusing and keep your eyes open. At this point, some people experience blurred vision while others report a misty effect. Experiences differ from person to person.
- Connect with your higher self by saying the trigger word *unity* (your agreement with your higher-self in chapter three) then state your intention. (For example, I intend to communicate with the spirit of my mother.)
- Tell yourself how you want to feel when you finish the RISCH™ session, ie, *After my session with Spirit, I'm going to feel wonderfully relaxed and calm.* Also give yourself a suggestion to emerge from hypnosis if anything untoward should happen. For example, you might suggest: *During this session should anything unexpected happen that requires my attention, I will instantly emerge from trance feeling fully alert and refreshed.* Focus your thoughts on the person you want to speak with. Create an image of that person in your mind. Make the image as clear as possible until you can practically see their features. If you have a difficult time visualizing, try feeling their presence. (Actually, it's a good idea to do both if you can.)
- Ask your questions. Do not force answers, but remain open to receiving information through any of your Clair abilities.
- Prior to emerging from your hypnotic trance, give yourself the posthypnotic suggestion: *From now on, every time I practice RISCH™ I will find it easier and easier to go into trance, and my experience with Spirit will be deeper and more rewarding.*
- When you are ready to end your session, thank your higher self and Spirit for the experience. Count yourself back to full awareness using 3-2-1. As you open your eyes take three deep, belly breaths, wiggle your fingers, and toes, and have a good stretch.
- Write down your impressions in a journal dedicated to Spirit communication

If you feel you're not getting a connection, it isn't because your loved one is upset with you or too busy to talk. You may have to attempt communication several times before you are successful. Also, it's very important to trust the impressions you receive.

~ 8 ~

POPULAR WAYS TO CONTINUE BONDS

"Memory sustains man in the world of life."
—Rabbi Samuel David Luzzatto

Continuing the Bond

Continuing a bond with a deceased loved one does not mean that you are living in the past. Our deceased loved ones are both present and absent. The bond we establish with the deceased will shift and take new forms over time, but the connection will always be there. Although the connection remains, we can choose to keep the bonds active or let them rest with the deceased. Most people feel that their continued bond with the deceased isn't valid unless it is legitimized through ritual. In addition to periodically setting aside some time to communicate with your loved one through the RISCH™ method, there are many other ways to legitimize your continued bond with a deceased loved one. The following list includes the most popular ways.

- Talk to them throughout the day;
- Allow yourself to feel their presence;
- Write letters to them;
- Write about them in your journal or diary;
- Display mementos and pictures of them where they can be seen by other people;
- Include them as part of special events and occasions;
- Imagine what advice they might give you when making tough decisions;
- Talk about them with new people who never got a chance to know your loved one;
- Live your life in a way you know they would be proud of;
- Take a trip they always wanted to take;

- Finish a project they never got to finish;
- Take-up a hobby they enjoyed;
- Periodically make their favorite meal;
- Keep a item of theirs that has significance for you;
- Plan for their death anniversary;
- Maintain their facebook page;
- Visit their grave or memorial site;
- Do an activity, alone or with someone else, that you always did together;
- Light a candle in their memory when you are missing them;
- Donate to their favorite charity or start a scholarship in their honor.

Talking to Them Throughout the Day

Talking to a deceased loved one is a very healthy way to cope with their death because it allows you the space and time to be present with them. Talking to them can help give you an opportunity to get closure on any issues that were left unresolved. It also allows you to acknowledge the fact that they are still with you in spirit form.

Allow Yourself To Feel Their Presence

It is common to feel the presence of your deceased loved one. According to research studies, feeling your loved one's presence has been shown to ease the sadness that accompanies grief. Allowing yourself to feel your loved one's presence is a normal and healthy way to continue bonds with them. The reason you feel their presence is because they are with you.

Write Letters to Them

The act of writing helps most people to cope with the emotions and thoughts associated with the loss of their loved one. Writing allows us to focus on our feelings at a deeper level, and releases the stress experienced by holding those feelings in. It also allows you to freely and safely express yourself to your deceased loved one without the fear of judgment or reprisal from other family members. Telling your deceased loved one exactly how you feel about certain adverse situations or events that occurred with them while they were alive may help you resolve any conflicted emotions you have, which will ultimately allow you to move forward in healing your grief. You can keep the letters or get rid of them.

Write About Them in Your Journal or Diary

In your journal, you can write anything about your deceased loved that you choose to. Some of the things people like to write about are:

Display Mementos or Photos of Them Where They Can be Seen by Other People

This may seem absurdly obvious, but there will be people who make you feel uncomfortable about keeping photos. For example, a woman who wrote in to Ask Amy expressing concern that her widowed boyfriend still had pictures of his wife around. She didn't ask our opinion, but luckily we decided to share what we thought anyway. Keeping photos around keeps us connected with our loved one and often helps us remember the ways that person continues to influence our lives.

Include Them as Part of Special Events and Occasions

Consider leaving an empty chair at holiday meals to honor your loved one, or using one of our 18 other suggestions. Discuss as a family other ways that you may want to involve your loved one's memory at special events. You will certainly be thinking of them on these big days, so there is no reason to keep that inside if you want to find a more open way to involve your loved one in the event. Organize gatherings on special days, such as their birthday. The holidays and special days can be difficult without a loved one's physical presence. Help make these days a little easier by organizing a gathering to honor your loved one's memory, such as a dinner. Everyone can bring a dish to pass and share memories of your loved one.

Imagine What Advice They Might Give You When Making Tough Decisions

Big decisions are often overwhelming and when you have lost the person who you would have talked it over with it can be especially hard. Imagining a conversation with them, what they would have said, and the advice they might have given can help us feel connected and also help make big life choices a little easier.

Talk About Them With New People Who Never Got a Chance To Know Your Loved One

There will often be new and important people in your life who did not know your loved one. It may be new friends, a significant other, or children, who never had the opportunity to meet your loved one when they were alive.

Keep your loved one's memory alive by sharing stories about them with your loved ones. Everyone has different experiences with a loved one that others would love to hear. Even if they didn't know the deceased, you can still tell them about who they were and how they positively influenced many lives, including your own.

Live Your Life In a Way You Know They Would Be Proud Of

Be it a spouse, a parent, grandparent, child, or friend, we often struggle knowing our loved one won't be there for accomplishments and milestones. Taking time to recognize that your loved one would be proud of you for a specific accomplishment can be comforting and remind us how we continue to be connected to our loved one.

Take a Trip They Always Wanted to Take

Though this one may sound depressing, I have known many grievers who have found comfort in this. Death can make us realize that life is short. We may ourselves be feeling inspired to travel and this can help us travel in a way that is meaningful in our grief. On trips like this, we may feel close to our loved one, imagining how they would have felt about the trip. It can be tough, certainly bittersweet, but for some people comforting. Another way to feel close to them is to travel to their favorite places. It doesn't have to be far away destinations. Even just going to their favorite restaurant or local coffee shop can create a continued bond. Another idea is to travel somewhere that they always wanted to go.

Finish a Project They Never Got to Finish

Be it a project around the house, a piece of artwork, a team they coached, or a volunteer project they were involved in, consider picking up where they left off. This can help you learn new things about your loved one, continue your connection with them in the present, and continue their legacy. Did your loved one start a project that they never finished? Why not take the opportunity to finish it for them? Doing this can help you feel closer to them. Or, you can start a project that they always wanted to do.

Take up a Hobby They Enjoyed

This one may push you out of your comfort zone, but if they loved to knit, learn to knit. If they loved to garden, learn to garden. It may not end up being the right fit for you, but either way, people often feel a closeness with their loved one in the process.

Periodically Make Their Favorite Meal

Making a recipe your loved one always made, or eating one of your loved one's favorite foods can bring back great memories and continue to connect us to our loved ones in everyday activities, like cooking and eating.

Keep an Item of Theirs That Has Significance for You

You can't keep everything (even though sometimes it is very hard to part with items!) but keep a few meaningful items can be extremely powerful. This could be an item they owned or an item they gave you. Either way, there can be comfort found in these items, as they make us feel close to our loved one.

Plan for Their Death Anniversary

Though it may feel like everyone else has moved on, you should not feel embarrassed or self-conscious about planning something in memory of your loved on each year on the anniversary of their death, or another special day. Be it a small, personal ritual or a large event, find something that works for you.

Maintain Their Facebook Page

This practice is becoming more and more common. Facebook has installed an application that will allow you to create a memorialization page for your deceased loved one. Maintaining a memorialization Facebook page allows the deceased person's friends and family an opportunity to express their continued bond.

Visit Their Grave or Memorial Site

A simple way to create a continued bond is to visit their gravesite or memorial location. You can leave flowers, talk to them, or simply sit and think about your loved one.

Do an Activity, Alone or With Someone Else, That You Always Did Together

Continue to do an activity that you always did together. Whether it was going to a holiday movie every year or baking cookies for your community's annual fundraiser, don't stop doing the traditions that were meaningful to you and your loved one.

Light A Candle in Their Memory When You Are Missing Them

Lighting a candle in honor of a loved one is a powerful ritual, especially during the holiday season or on a day when you're missing them a little more than usual. After lighting the candle, take a few moments and bask in the warm glow while thinking about your loved one. This is a wonderful way to draw the spirit of your loved one to you when you need to feel their presence.

Donate to Their Favorite Charity or Start A Scholarship in Their Honor

Make a difference in someone's life by donating to a charitable cause or organization that your deceased loved one contributed to while they were alive. You can also create a scholarship in their honor. For instance, if your loved one was a nurse, start a scholarship in their memory to help support a nursing student.

Worksheet #1

Using the worksheet below, place a checkmark by the rituals you plan to use to continue the bond with your loved one. You may use any of the rituals already listed by placing a checkmark by it or create your own in the empty spaces. Be sure to include the frequency of your continue bond ritual, i.e., birthdays, at Christmas, etc.

Continuing Bonds Ritual	√	Frequency of Ritual (times, days or dates)
Talk To Them Throughout The Day		
Allow Yourself To Feel Their Presence		
Write Letters To Them		
Write About Them In Your Journal Or Diary		
Display Mementos Or Photos Of Them Where They Can Be Seen By Other People		
Include Them As Part Of Special Events And Occasions		
Imagine What Advice They Might Give You When Making Tough Decisions		
Talk About Them With New People Who Never Got A Chance To Know Your Loved One		
Live Your Life In A Way You Know They Would Be Proud Of		
Take A Trip They Always Wanted To Take		

Finish A Project They Never Got To Finish		
Take Up A Hobby They Enjoyed		
Periodically Make Their Favorite Meal		
Keep An Item Of Theirs That Has Significance For You		
Plan For Their Death Anniversary		
Maintain Their Facebook Page		
Visit Their Grave Or Memorial Site		
Do An Activity, Alone Or With Someone Else, That You Always Did Together		
Light A Candle In Their Memory When You Are Missing Them		
Donate To Their Favorite Charity Or Start A Scholarship In Their Honor		

Coping With Difficult Dates & Events

Certain dates are difficult because they are reminders of the fact that our deceased loved one will never again be physically present for special events such as weddings, graduations, births and more.

Although these dates are difficult, they also provide an opportunity to acknowledge, and include the spirit of your loved one in the event. There is also the opportunity for recalling and sharing cherished memories of the deceased loved one with other family members, and friends. The exercise below will help you focus on ways to cope with these difficult dates by including the spirit of your deceased loved one in the event.

Worksheet #2

Listed below are common dates bereaved people may find difficult. Create ways you can continue bonds with your deceased loved one by acknowledging the presence of their spirit in the event.

Event	Date	Come Up With A Way To Include The Spirit Of Your Loved One In The Event
Birthday of the loved one who died		
Your birthday		
Other birthdays		
Wedding anniversary		
Anniversary of the date of death		
Holidays (specify which ones)		
1		
2		
3		
4		
5		
6		
Graduation		
Wedding		

Birth of a baby		
Christening/Baptism		

Continuing bond rituals provide a way for you to continue having a relationship with your deceased loved one. This relationship can no longer be a physical one of flesh and blood, but it can be maintained as an active spiritual one. This spiritual relationship may involve perpetual conversations carried on in your mind with the deceased, or by setting aside specific times to communicate and received communication from them. It may also involve a sense of being watched over by them, as well as a need to include them in decision-making.

Maintaining a continued bond does not mean that you are denying that the death happened, that you are living in the past, or failing to adapt to the loss and move forward in restructuring your life. Research actually shows that maintaining a relationship with the deceased can be a strong motivator for healthy adjustment and eventually finding a new happiness again in life. In this way, the deceased and former life are never forgotten, but carried forward and integrated into the future.

~ 9 ~

COPING WITH GRIEF

"Who would have thought my shrivel'd heart could have recovered Greenness?"
—George Herbert

Grief is a Maelstrom

Grief is a maelstrom of difficult and overwhelming emotions we experience upon the death of a loved one. It's been said that grief is the price we pay for having loved another person. Many people mistakenly believe that grief is a single emotion, but normal acute grief is actually a multifaceted and uncontrollable response to the pain of loss. The most common emotions experienced are shock, anger, disbelief, guilt, and profound sadness. Although the emotional pain of acute grief is normal, it can be so intense that it negatively impacts your physical and cognitive health, making it difficult to eat, sleep, or even think straight.

The process of grieving can be thought of as a roller coaster ride. It is full of ups and downs, highs and lows. Sometimes we feel we are coping well, and other times we may fall apart at the slightest emotional trigger, or memory, which make us feel that we aren't coping well at all. Because each individual reacts to loss differently, there is a wide range of symptoms that may be experienced during acute grief. The following two lists contain the most common physical and cognitive symptoms of acute grief.

The following are common physical symptoms:

- tightening in the throat or chest;
- dizziness and shortness of breath;
- anxiety related chest pain (be sure to see a doctor for any type of chest pain you may be experiencing;A weakened immune system, making infection related illness more likely;
- sleeping too much or not enough;
- eating too much or not enough;

- extreme restlessness that is atypical for the individual (hyperactive, constantly moving from one activity to another, and restless leg syndrome);
- extreme sedentary behavior that is atypical for the individual (very low energy, no physical activity for long periods of time).

The following are common cognitive symptoms:

- experiencing gaps in memory;
- searching for their loved one even though they know their loved one has died;
- confusion, irritability, anxiety, and the inability to concentrate;
- odd and frightening dreams
- difficulty remembering;

Coping effectively with the death of a loved one is vital to your mental and physical health. The only way to heal grief is to allow yourself to process the emotions, and find purpose in living your life in the physical absence of your loved one.

Things You Can Do to Cope Effectively With Grief

Get Exercise

Exercise provides two wonderful benefits for people who are grieving. It provides a distraction from the cycle of negative thinking, and triggers the release of neurotransmitters called endorphins (endorphins relieve stress and pain, and can give you a feeling of euphoria). Both of these benefits help to prevent chronic depression. It can also help you sleep better, and improve your outlook on life. If you regularly exercised before the death of your loved one, then try to continue that routine as much as possible. If you have led a sedentary lifestyle, then consider finding some time to exercise each day. Taking your dog for a walk, riding your bike, or asking a friend to stroll with you in the local park or mall are excellent and practical ways to get your body in motion.

Choose Good Company

Look for friends, old and new, who know how grief feels and who can let you be "alone but not alone" when you just need company and who won't place any further burdens or expectations on you.

Be Gentle With Yourself

Try not to judge yourself for not "doing better" or "keeping it together." Grieving is a highly individual experience; there's no right or wrong way to grieve. How you grieve depends on many factors, including your personality and coping style, your life experience, your faith, and how significant the loss was to you. Everyone processes grief differently, and there is no perfect way to grieve. It will get easier as you adjust to living your life without the physical presence of your loved one.

Embrace All Emotions

Realize that the feelings associated with grief are normal, and you will experience them whether you like it or not. All you can do is acknowledge your feelings and work through them. Mindfulness is an excellent way to acknowledge and work through the avalanche of emotions related to grief. To be mindful is to become aware of your emotions, thoughts and sensations in the moment. When applied to the grieving process, mindfulness reminds you that your pain is temporary. By simply observing your grief as it exists in the present moment, you let go of the need to avoid the pain or obsess over your loss. Research has shown that engaging in mindfulness practices after suffering the loss of a loved one decreases the occurrence and intensity of depression and anxiety, and improves cognitive and memory function during the grief process. It's also important to know when to seek professional grief counseling. I'll discuss more about when to get professional help later in the chapter.

Set A Regular Sleep Schedule

Make it a goal to go to bed and awaken at the same time each day. Give yourself a good amount of time to rest, but be on guard for sleeping too much as a way to avoid the hard work of grieving. Physical and emotional exhaustion is common. Grief typically disrupts our normal sleep patterns, so getting proper rest is important. To whatever extent possible, try to develop a regular bedtime routine and schedule; minimize distractions, such as a television, iPad or tablet, or cell phone; and keep your bedroom dark. In addition, try to avoid caffeinated drinks for at least three hours before bedtime.

Join A Support Group

Joining a support group is a great way to engage in conversation, share what you're feeling, and gain perspective on what others are doing to cope with their loss. Grief support groups are commonly held at local mental health centers, community centers, and churches. Some of these groups have been made available online; however, it's my opinion that venturing out of the house to meet with other people who have a common interest has its own inherent therapeutic value.

Maintain Structure in Your Day and Keep Busy

This means getting out of the bed at the same time every day, dressing, and grooming, even if you are not leaving the house. You cannot dwell on your sorrow or your loss every waking moment. In the first flush of grief, you may feel you cannot control the extent of your suffering. But friends, activities, and other support can help to form a lifeline that gets you through the pain.

Set Goals

Set small, reachable, short-term goals so that you don't get overwhelmed.

Make a List of Daily Activities

This can help while you are grieving because forgetfulness is common.

Be Cautious About Making Big Decisions

Many grief counselors and business advocates will advise you not make any major decisions or changes in home or work within the first six months of the death of your spouse or partner. Grief can feel overwhelming and inescapable, so it's easy to understand the urge to simplify your financial situation or make immediate changes in your life to escape memories. However, in the aftermath of your loss, you may not be thinking clearly enough to make rapid decisions. Reacting out of fear is usually not wise. For example, selling your home right away might offer an escape from the reminders of your loved one, but remaining there might prove more financially advantageous in the long run. Likewise, keeping existing credit card accounts or an automobile with a lender lien might help you establish your creditworthiness sooner.

Take Care of Your Spiritual Needs

Find time, whether through a spiritual practice or a creative outlet, to connect to things that give you inspiration and help you maintain your sense of meaning and purpose. Religious or spiritual beliefs may also help by providing a larger meaning to a loved one's life and death. For some, the belief that a loved one is enjoying the blessings of heaven or preparing for their next life by reincarnating helps to ease the pain of grief. Also, belief that loved ones are watching over you, to protect and guide you, as well as the belief that you will be reunited in another place after your own death can help ease the pain of grief. If prayer helps to sustain you, set aside time for it. If you are a religious person, it may be beneficial for you to read spiritual texts that bring you comfort, attend church services, and share your circumstances with your minister who can help you place the death in the context of your faith. For some people, gardening or communing with nature is soothing and offers an opportunity to observe and appreciate the rhythms of life and death in the natural world. Meditation and yoga may also beneficial in easing grief because they calm the mind and promote a sense of well being.

Stay Hydrated and Eat Properly

Drink plenty of water throughout the day and avoid excessive alcohol consumption, which acts as a diuretic and can actually dehydrate your body. While grieving, some people often find it difficult to have a balanced, and nutritious meal. Either they feel hungry, but don't want to eat alone or they don't feel hungry at all. Regardless, it's vitally important to your health and well being that you make an effort to eat nourishing foods. You may find it easier to eat small amounts of healthy snacks and nutritious foods frequently throughout the day. Allow yourself some empty calorie comfort food if you must, but keep in mind the importance of promoting and maintaining your immune system with good, wholesome food. Your immune system protects your body against things that can make you sick. The experience of grief can significantly weaken the immune system.

Talk to Your Doctor

It's important to keep all of your doctor appointments and be sure to tell your doctor how your reaction to grief is impacting your life so he or she can help you with strategies to initiate and maintain good health habits.

Plan for Life Event Triggers

While you may have been able to navigate through all the stages of grief, know that there may be "triggers" in the near future that may bring all those emotions rushing back once more. Typically, life milestones may remind you of a loss like holidays, birthdays, anniversaries or some other special event. Here is where families and friends can again lend support so call on them. Most likely, they will be thinking about those moments too and will be wondering how you feel. Have a plan where you can turn these "triggers" into positive moments, such as a celebration or time to meditate on the happiness you enjoyed together before the loss.

Keep a Journal

Some feelings may be too hard to speak aloud, like anger or regret; expressing them on paper can be freeing. Journal writing can serve as a release as well as a meaningful expression of yourself, and allows a private way to work through the many emotions experienced during the journey of grief.

Fun Things for Me to Do While I'm Grieving

It is easy to lose track of the things that bring us joy when we are grief stricken. Participating in fun activities provides us with the distraction we need to take a mental break from the intense feelings of sadness associated with grief. Having fun also helps us to focus on the importance of pursuing and enjoying our own life to the fullest.

I have included the following list to give you an idea of things you can do to have fun while you are working through your grief. For the exercise below, you can choose from the following list or come up with your own ways of having fun:

- take art lessons,
- take sewing lessons,
- take cooking lessons,
- take a jewelry making workshop,
- watch favorite sports program on t.v.,
- take a short weekend trip,
- join a book club,
- write a book,
- invite friends and/or family over for dinner and a movie,
- go to the symphony,
- attend a community theater play,
- attend the opera,
- go to a baseball, football, basketball or hockey game,
- plant new vegetables or flowers in your garden,
- cook out or go on a picnic,
- join a gym,
- have a game night and invite others,
- go to the movies alone or with others,
- go out for dinner alone or with a others,
- adopt a pet,
- get a new hairdo or hair color,
- make a scrapbook for your memories,
- make a vision board of your reorganized life,
- shop for memorialization items,
- make a shadow box,
- visit museums and local historical places,
- buy yourself flowers and chocolates,
- take dance lessons,
- listen to music,
- join a new club,
- attend spiritual or religious services,
- explore a new hobby,
- go shopping at the farmer's market,
- spend time with children or grandchildren,
- go out for ice cream alone or with others,
- bake brownies or cookies for yourself or a neighbor,
- go hiking,

- take golf lessons,
- take a special golfing trip,
- take photos of nature,
- watch the sun rise or set,
- watch funny movies,
- buy new furniture,
- spend time with a friend you haven't seen in a long time,
- browse a bookstore and buy a new book,
- go horseback riding,
- try a new food you've never had before,
- make vacation plans,
- take a step toward achieving a long desired goal such as starting a new business or returning to school,
- join a new community or meetup group,
- teach an art or craft that you enjoy doing,
- volunteer for or organize a charitable cause,
- take a course in a subject that interests you,
- learn a new language,
- start or participate in a blog,
- travel to a new place and explore it alone or with others,
- go shopping for a new outfit,
- participate in a cause you believe in,
- participate in Yoga,
- take a course in meditation or mindfulness,
- travel to a fun destination alone or with others,
- go for a bike ride.

Worksheet # 3

Take some time and write down activities you feel may be fun for you to do alone or with a friend or family member. You may use the activities listed above or come up with some of your own.

Fun Activities For Me To Do Within The Next Few Months	Alone? (Yes/No)	Name Of Family Member/ Friend I Can Do This With
1		
2		
3		

4			
5			
6			
7			
8			
9			
10			
11			
12			
13			
14			

Grief is an intensely personal process. Accept that it follows no magic formula or time frame. It will take as long as it takes. Be careful not to take on responsibilities beyond what is realistic, and be sure to participate in activities that bring you enjoyment.

Restructuring Your Life After the Death of a Loved One

Life will be different and sometimes difficult; but, you can continue a bond with the person who has died if you choose to. A lessening in the intensity of grief is not the end of the attachment to your loved one. It just signals that you are focusing on and moving forward with your own life. Death does not necessarily end a bond. Each individual must decide how the bond will be continued. There is also nothing wrong with the choice to sever a bond with a deceased, especially if it helps you to move forward with your own life.

At some point during the grief process, you'll realize that the death of your loved one has changed your life, and you'll gradually start to create a new one. Restructuring your life can actually give you the strength you need to continue to cope with your loss. Finding purpose and meaning in your life, especially after the death of a spouse, begins with identifying what's meaningful to you. Creating goals for your life is an excellent way to begin the restructuring process. A goal statement will help you to identify and set goals for achieving those things that are important to you in your restructured life. Implementing new rituals and daily habits that will allow you to achieve the goals of your new life are a vital part of this blueprint. Setting a goal and being able to achieve it will help you see that you still have control over some things. Reaching the goal will hopefully help to bring back some of your old confidence. Be sure to include goals in your blueprint that will allow you to have new and joyful experiences in your new life. If you're a widow or widower and miss the experience of intimacy and the sharing your life with another, then set a goal that when are ready, you will find love again. No one needs to know about your goal-setting and future plans. The last thing you want to do is risk criticism and judgments which will only add to your grief. Remember, this is your restructured life, and only you have the right to create it. Over time as you process your grief, you may want to modify your blueprint. Be sure to focus on what you want to experience in your life. Don't let yourself be made to feel that you are somehow betraying your deceased loved one, or are being selfish for having a new life. I have listed some popular examples of goal statements you can use in the exercise below, or you can create your own. Either way, the objective of this exercise is to get you moving forward with your life.

Popular Goal Statements

I Will Get Up, Get Dressed, and Head Out Each Day With The Intent of Interacting With Other People to Decrease my Feelings of Loneliness & Isolation

This goal is especially important for widows and widowers who are retired, and may be living alone. Make it a point each day to get up, get dressed, and get out of the house. When figuring out where to go and what to do each day, look for interesting and engaging activities that provide an opportunity for conversation and interaction with other people.

I Will Take a Road Trip Each Month to a Destination That Is Exciting to Me so That I Can Allow Myself to Experience New & Pleasurable Adventures

There is no right or wrong way when working through your grief and bereavement. Planning and taking a road trip can be a life-changing experience when dealing with the loss of a significant loved one. The time away from your everyday life can help ease the pain of your despair by allowing you to see and experience things outside of your usual surroundings.

I Will Get Exercise Every Day Because It Is Important for Me to Take Care Of Myself & Be Healthy

Daily exercise is a wonderful way to overcome the physical and mental fatigue associated with grieving. A short daily walk helps clear your mind and create more mood-elevating chemicals in your brain. Set a goal to get some kind of physical activity everyday.

Everyday for The Next Week I Will Identify Something Positive About Myself in My New Role That Will Help Me Appreciate Just Being Me

Rediscovering yourself can feel like starting all over again, especially if you lost a spouse. You'll have to learn how to assume a role that is no longer identified as that of a husband or wife. Through your loss, you've gained an opportunity to reinvent yourself and reshape your life into something different. Be sure to take advantage of opportunities that will bring you true happiness and enjoyment.

Everyday I Will Make The Choice to Live a Full & Meaningful Life so I Can Move Forward And Find Enjoyment

Permitting yourself find joy after a crushing period of grief does not mean you have forgotten your loved one or the situation. Many people prolong their suffering because they feel guilty or believe they are selfish if they choose to be happy again. It's vitally important to give the same compassion and empathy towards yourself that you would extend to others. Restructuring your life is a gradual process, so allow yourself as much time as you need.

Setting Effective Restructuring Goals

Setting restructuring goals can help you to intentionally move forward with life on your own terms and in a way that will bring you personal fulfillment. Effective goal setting is essential to achieving your goal. The SMART method of goal setting allows you to set your goals in a simple, but very effective way. A SMART goal is: Specific, Measurable, Attainable, Relevant, and Time Oriented. The following statement is an example of a smart goal: "Every weekend I will attend at least one social function that will allow me the opportunity interact with other people." An example of a goal statement that isn't smart is: "I will attend social gatherings." This goal isn't smart because it doesn't have a time frame, nor does it identify why the goal is needed. The table below explains what a smart goal is and how to write one.

Table #1

Specify What You Want	• This is your goal statement. • It should spell out exactly what you want and why you want to achieve it. • Use verbs to express physical or mental action, as much as possible.

Measurable	• This is where you set parameters for achieving your goal. • This helps you identify if your goal was accomplished. • It can be qualitative, but is usually quantitative.
Attainable	• These are the resources and activities you will implement to achieve your goal. Activities You Will Implement
Relevant	• Make sure your goal related activities actually help you to achieve the outcome you desire.
Time Based	• Specify a reasonable period of time for your goal to be accomplished.

Exercise #4

Use the above table to guide you formulating goal statements that will help you start restructuring your life. I have added a goal statement to get you started.

Specific	Measurable	Attainable	Relevant	Time Based
1) I will actively participate in a grief support group once a week for the next twelve weeks.	My goal will be achieved as evidenced by my active participation in the support group for twelve weeks.	I will meet with the group on either Monday or Wednesday night because I am available.	Participating in a grief support group will give me an outlet to share my grief and to learn how other people cope with their grief.	**My goal was achieved:** I actively participated every week in a twelve-week grief support group, and I was able to share my grief and learn how other people cope with their grief.

2)

3)

4)

Complicated Grief

Grief is a usually a short-term phenomenon known as acute grief, although the pain may return unexpectedly at a later time. In some situations, an individual may experience prolonged grief in which they have significant distress long after the loss occurred. This is known as complicated grief, lasting months or years. Without appropriate grief therapy, such grief can create great dysfunction in an individual's life causing isolation, chronic loneliness, and ultimately failure to thrive. Common signs of complicated grief are:

- Having trouble carrying out activities of daily living;
- No longer wishing to participate in social activities;
- Feeling depressed or deeply sad all of the time;
- Blaming yourself or feel guilty for the death of your loved one;
- Believing that you did something wrong or could have prevented the death;
- Feeling like you've lost your sense of purpose in life;
- Feeling life isn't worth living anymore;
- Feeling that part of yourself has died;
- Loss of a sense of control, security, or trust;
- Excessive irritability bitterness, or anger related to the death;
- Feelings of numbness and detachment;
- Inability to think about the loss with any positive memories;
- Intense or persistent longing or pining for the deceased person;
- Intense sorrow or pain over the loss;

- Inability to focus on anything but the loved one's death;
- Extreme focus (to the exclusion of other facets of life) on things that remind you of your lost loved one.

If you have been unsuccessful at processing grief on your own, and find that it is interfering with your ability to lead a full life, or carry on with the activities of daily living, then it may be time to see a Grief Therapist. This mental health professional has the qualifications to help you view things from a healthy perspective so that you can move forward with your life. While Grief Counselors are wonderful in helping you get through acute grief, Grief Therapists are the only ones who can provide you with the level of therapy you need to deal with complicated grief. Many Grief Therapist will see you without a referral from a primary care provider; however, it is also a good idea to contact your primary doctor about your complicated grief. This way, they can collaborate with your counselor and prescribe any medication you might need to help you cope. Also, if you are interested in counseling, but prefer not to go into an office setting, there are online resources available that could be beneficial for you.

OTHER BOOKS BY SHIRLEY SMOLKO I

Spirits Everywhere!
Shirley Smolko

A practicing Registered Nurse for close to three decades, Shirley Smolko—The Venetian Medium—is also a gifted Psychic Medium who has communicated with Spirit from the time she was five years old. In this captivating book, Shirley shares her most fascinating stories about the spirits she has encountered inhabiting the ethers everywhere. *My Adventures as a Psychic Nurse & Medium: Spirits Everywhere!* Is a scary good read that will keep you glued to each and every page.

OTHER BOOKS BY SHIRLEY SMOLKO II

Over the years hospitals have been perceived as havens of hope, healing, and birth. They have also been perceived as prisons of pain, suffering, and death. Because of the large number of deaths that occur at hospitals each day, it should come as no surprise that hospitals are very haunted. The earthbound souls that haunt hospitals may become trapped because they are confused, have unfinished business, are afraid of what awaits them on the other side, or are hungry for physical life and looking for someone they can easily possess to fulfill their fleshy desires. Regardless of the reasons spirits become trapped, these wayward souls can be found in every corridor and room inside a hospital. Hospitals are very haunted and I should know because I am a psychic nurse! Join me on my adventures into the fascinating world of spirits and haunted hospitals. After reading *My Adventures as a Psychic Nurse & Medium: Haunted Hospitals!* you may find yourself too scared to enter another hospital.

www.ingramcontent.com/pod-product-compliance
Lightning Source LLC
Chambersburg PA
CBHW081154070526
44583CB00021B/2837